ALGEBRA 1
WORD PROBLEMS

Written by Anita Harnadek

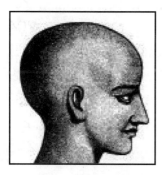

© 2001
CRITICAL THINKING BOOKS & SOFTWARE
www.criticalthinking.com
P.O. Box 448 • Pacific Grove • CA 93950-0448
Phone 800-458-4849 • FAX 831-393-3277
ISBN 0-89455-799-8
Printed in the United States of America

TABLE OF CONTENTS

INTRODUCTION

Most of us have trouble solving word problems. And we have even more trouble solving algebra word problems.

But there are some things we can learn about algebra word problems to make them easier to solve.

The next 26 pages contain seven lessons:

Lesson 1: Many verbs can be replaced by "=."

Lesson 2: Think about what your equations say.

Lesson 3: Take the problem step by step.

Lesson 4: Check your solutions.

Lesson 5: Think about the nature of the thing the problem talks about.

Lesson 6: Use your common sense.

Lesson 7: If all else fails, try the "wild guess" method.

Each lesson contains examples and practice problems. Your own algebra book will give you other problems to work.

Don't worry if the problems in your own algebra book seem different than the ones here. The same ideas apply to all algebra word problems.

HOW TO SOLVE ALGEBRA WORD PROBLEMS

LESSON 1:

MANY VERBS CAN BE REPLACED BY "="

Verbs can often be replaced by "=."

Example 1.1:

<u>Statement</u>: Bruno's age is four years more than Mark's age.

<u>Algebraic statement</u>:

Put B = Bruno's age (in years) now.

Put M = Mark's age (in years) now.

Then $M + 4$ is 4 years more than Mark's age now.

So Bruno's age is $M + 4$.

So B is $M + 4$.

So

$B = M + 4$.

Example 1.2:

<u>Statement</u>: Sue is twice as old as Nancy was two years ago.

<u>Algebraic statement</u>:

Put S = Sue's age (in years) now.

Put N = Nancy's age (in years) now.

Then $N - 2$ = Nancy's age (in years) 2 years ago.

So S is twice as much as $N - 2$.

So

$S = 2(N - 2)$.

Example 1.3:

Statements: The sum of two numbers is 97. One of the numbers is 5 more than the other.

Algebraic statements:

Put s = the smaller number.

Put l = the larger number.

Then $s + l$ is the sum of the two numbers.

So $s + l$ is 97.

So

$s + l = 97.$

Now look at the second given statement. The larger number has to be the one that is 5 more than the other.

So l is 5 more than s.

So l is $s + 5$.

So

$l = s + 5.$

So the two equations are

$s + l = 97$

$l = s + 5$

PRACTICE PROBLEMS FOR LESSON 1

Write an equation for each statement.

1. Margot's age is five years more than June's age.

2. Tyler is seven years older than Jones.

3. Evans is three years younger than Wilson.

4. Jack has two more marbles than Ruth.

5. Iris has twice as many marbles as Antonio.

6. Chocolate costs 60¢ more a pound than peanut brittle.

7. Ben's test score was 10 points higher than Amana's.

8. Norm weighs 5 pounds more than Jon.

9. The sum of two numbers is 54. One of the numbers is 8 more than the other.

10. The sum of two numbers is 47. One of the numbers is 19 less than the other.

LESSON 2:

THINK ABOUT WHAT YOUR EQUATIONS SAY

Another reason we sometimes have trouble solving algebra word problems is that we don't stop to think about what we're writing.

Example 2.1:

Write an equation to show how many feet, f, are in y yards.

We are to use these variables:

f = no. of feet

y = no. of yards

Now 3 feet is 1 yard. So do we write

$3f = y$?

No! Think about it. This says we multiply the number of feet by 3 to get the number of yards. It says that 1 foot is 3 yards. Instead, the equation should be

$3y = f.$

This says we take the number of yards and multiply by 3 to get the number of feet.

Example 2.2:

Write an equation to show the number of ice cubes, c, in t trays, each of which holds sixteen ice cubes.

One tray holds sixteen ice cubes, so do we have

$t = 16c$?

No! We have

$c = 16t.$

PRACTICE PROBLEMS FOR LESSON 2

Write an equation to show how many

1. inches, *i*, are in *f* feet.

2. months, *m*, are in *y* years.

3. years, *y*, are in *m* months.

4. seconds, *s*, are in *h* hours.

5. centimeters, *c*, are in *m* meters.

6. 24-ounce cans of tomato paste, *c*, can be filled from *o* ounces of tomato paste.

7. liters, *l*, are in *m* milliliters.

8. packages of paper, *p*, each containing 500 sheets, can be made from *s* sheets of paper.

9. teachers, *t*, will be needed for *s* students if the average teacher instructs 26 students.

10. feet, *f*, are in *m* miles.

LESSON 3:

TAKE THE PROBLEM STEP BY STEP

One reason given for having trouble with algebra word problems is, "I don't know where to start!"

Starting is easy.

1a.   Decide what number is unknown.

1b.   Choose a variable to represent this number.

1c.   Write a sentence to explain the variable clearly.

Example 3.1 (beginning):

Four years ago, Bob was one-third as old as he is now. How old is Bob?

We will now apply steps 1a, 1b, and 1c in order:

1a.   The question asks for Bob's age now, so we'll say that this is the unknown number.

1b.   Choose B as the variable.

1c.   Put B = Bob's age (in years) now.

- Notice we did not write, "B = Bob." (Bob is not the number that is unknown.)

- Notice we included "(in years)" in the sentence. [If the problem talked about months instead of years, we would write "(in months)".]

- Notice we included the word "now" in the sentence. [Without "now," the sentence would read, "B = Bob's age (in years)." Then we might wonder if B stood for Bob's age now, or Bob's age 4 years ago.]

You can see that we are very fussy about the way we start on a problem. But now our thinking is clear and we can go ahead with the next steps.

2a.   See what is said about things relating to the unknown number.

2b.   Write statements describing these things.

EXAMPLE 3.1 (middle):

Four years ago, Bob was one-third as old as he is now. How old is Bob?

We continue with step 1c, and we add steps 2a and 2b.

1c.   Put B = Bob's age (in years) now.

2a.   Bob's age four years ago is talked about.

2b.   Four years ago, Bob was younger than he is now. So his age was less than it is now. So $B - 4$ = Bob's age (in years) four years ago.

All right, what do we have so far? We have these statements:

1c. B = Bob's age (in years) now.

2b. $B - 4$ = Bob's age (in years) four years ago.

So far, so good. Now for the final steps in setting up the equations to solve:

3a.   See how the expressions we have are related.

3b.   Set up the equation(s) to be solved.

EXAMPLE 3.1 (end):

Four years ago, Bob was one-third as old as he is now. How old is Bob?

Now we repeat steps 1c and 2b, and we add steps 3a and 3b.

1c.   Put B = Bob's age (in years) now.

2b.   Then $B - 4$ = Bob's age (in years) four years ago.

3a.   The expressions we have are B and $B - 4$. There is a relation of one-third between these two expressions.

3b.   Now where does the one-third go? To decide, we read the problem again.

"Four years ago" refers to "Bob's age four years ago." So that's $B - 4$. So the problem says, "$B - 4$ was one-third of Bob's age now." So that's $B - 4$ = one-third of B. So

$$B - 4 = \frac{1}{3}B.$$

SUMMARY

1.   Decide what number is unknown.

     Choose a variable to represent this number.

     Write a clear explanation of this variable.

2.   See what the problem says about things relating to the variable.

     Write statements describing these things.

3.   See how the problem relates the expressions in steps 1 and 2.

     Set up the equation(s) to be solved.

EXAMPLE 3.2:

Manuel is five years older than Jenny. Jenny is three-fourths as old as Manuel. How old is Manuel? How old is Jenny?

1.   Put M = Manuel's age (in years) now.

     Put J = Jenny's age (in years) now.

2. $J + 5$ = five years more than Jenny's age (in years) now.

     $\frac{3}{4}M$ = three-fourths of Manuel's age (in years) now.

3. $M = J + 5$

     $J = \frac{3}{4}M$

EXAMPLE 3.3:

Four years ago, Bea was one-third as old as she will be eight years from now. How old is Bea?

1.   Put B = Bea's age (in years) now.

2. $B - 4$ = Bea's age (in years) four years ago.

     $B + 8$ = Bea's age (in years) eight years from now.

     $\frac{1}{3}(B + 8)$ = one-third of Bea's age eight years from now.

3. $B - 4 = \frac{1}{3}(B + 8)$

PRACTICE PROBLEMS FOR LESSON 3

Explain each variable. Write the equation(s) needed to solve each problem.

1. Harry is half as old as Mort. Mort is seven years older than Harry. How old is each boy?

2. June has twice as many marbles as Norm. Norm has nine marbles fewer than June. How many marbles does each person have?

3. Ann is two years older than Barry, who is five years younger than Cal. Cal is twice as old as Ann. How old is each person?

4. Mali has thirty cents more than Chet, who has three-fourths as much money as Mali. How much does each person have?

5. One kind of candy sells for 90¢ more a pound than another kind. A pound of each sells for a total of $5.10. What is the selling price of each kind?

　　　　9

6. A soft drink sells for 20¢ more than the deposit required on the bottle. The cost of the soft drink and the bottle deposit totals 70¢. How much is the soft drink? The bottle deposit?

7. Terry is twice as old as Urania, who is three times as old as Sam, who is ten years younger than Terry. How old is Urania?

8. The medium size of a product costs 40¢ more than the small size. The small size costs one-third as much as the large size. The large size costs 90¢ more than the medium size. What is the cost of each size?

9. Jones has received a raise of $1000 each year for the last five years, and she will continue to receive such raises for each of the next ten years. Four years ago, she made one-fourth as much money as she will make five years from now. How much does she make now?

LESSON 4:

CHECK YOUR SOLUTIONS

It doesn't do much good to set up an equation and solve it if the answer doesn't work in the given problem.

EXAMPLE 4.1:

Four years ago, Bob was one-third as old as he is now. How old is Bob?

Suppose we goof up and have this equation:

$$\frac{1}{3}(B - 4) = B$$

Solving, we get $B = -2$, and this works in our equation.

The trouble is, it doesn't work in the given problem.

First, Bob can't be –2 years old.

Second, even if he could be, –2 still doesn't work. If he's –2 now, then he was –6 four years ago. And –6 is not one-third of –2.

Once we set up our equation(s) and solve them, <u>we must always check our answers by seeing if they work in the given problem.</u>

Sometimes we can set up the right equation(s) to solve a problem and still get a wrong answer.

EXAMPLE 4.2:

I am thinking of a positive number. Eight less than this number multiplied by fifteen more than this number is zero. What is the number?

Put n = the given number.

Then $(n - 8)(n + 15) = 0$.

Solving, we get two answers:

$n = 8$, and $n = -15$.

Notice that both answers work in the equation. But the given problem says that the number is positive. So $n = -15$ does not work in the given problem.

So the only solution is $n = 8$.

EXAMPLE 4.3:

A rectangle is 7 cm longer than it is wide. Its area is 120 sq cm. What are its dimensions?

Put l = length (cm) of the given rectangle.

Put w = width (cm) of the given rectangle.

Then $l = w + 7$

$wl = 120$

Solving, we get w = 8 or w = –15. So the width can be 8 or –15. But wait. A rectangle can't have a negative width. So w = –15 doesn't work in the given problem.

So $w = 8$.

Then $l = w + 7$, so $l = 15$.

PRACTICE PROBLEMS FOR LESSON 4

Go back to the practice problems for Lesson 3 (pages 10 and 11). Solve the equations and see whether or not the answers work in the given problems.

1. Do problem 1.   6. Do problem 6.

2. Do problem 2.   7. Do problem 7.

3. Do problem 3.   8. Do problem 8.

4. Do problem 4.   9. Do problem 9.

5. Do problem 5.

LESSON 5:

THINK ABOUT THE NATURE OF THE THING
THE PROBLEM TALKS ABOUT

Sometimes we have trouble with algebra word problems just because we don't use what we know about how things work.

EXAMPLE 5.1:

A boat moves against the current at one speed. Using the same effort, it moves with the current at another speed. We have to find the boat's speed in still water. What variables do we use, and what expressions do we use?

> Think about the nature of a boat in water. What happens when it goes against the current? (It goes slower than it goes in still water.) What happens when it goes with the current? (It goes faster than it goes in still water.)

So:

Put b = the speed of the boat in still water.

Put c = the speed of the current.

Then

$b + c$ = the speed of the boat when it moves with the current.

And

$b - c$ = the speed of the boat when it moves against the current.

EXAMPLE 5.2:

The sum of the digits of a two-digit number is 7. When the digits are reversed, the result is 27 more than the given number. What is the given number?

Choose some two-digit number and think about it. Choose 37, for instance. How are 3 and 7 related so that the result is 37? [We write numbers so that 3 is called "the tens' digit" and 7 is called "the units' digit." So 37 = 10(3) + 7.]

Now we're ready to tackle the problem.

Put t = the tens' digit of the given number.

Put u = the units' digit of the given number.

Then $10t + u$ = the given number.

The problem says we add the digits. The digits are t and u, so we have

$t + u = 7.$

Now what about the second sentence? What do we have when we reverse the digits? Take 37 again. We get 73 when we reverse the digits.

So instead of 10(3) + 7, we have 10(7) + 3. So the given number, $10t + u$, becomes $10u + t$ when the digits are reversed.

So the second sentence says that $10u + t$ is 27 more than $10t + u$.

That is, $10u + t = 27 + 10t + u.$

So our two equations for this problem are

$t + u = 7$

$10u + t = 27 + 10t + u.$

EXAMPLE 5.3:

Sue has three more dimes than nickels. The total is worth 90¢. How many dimes does she have? How many nickels?

<u>Wrong solution</u>:

The unthinking person writes this:

d = dimes
n = nickels
$d = n + 3$
$d + n = 90$

We solve the equations and get $43\frac{1}{2}$ nickels and $46\frac{1}{2}$ dimes. And these answers satisfy the equations. But even if we could have half a coin, the answers don't check out with the problem, because the total value of $43\frac{1}{2}$ nickels and $46\frac{1}{2}$ dimes is not 90¢. So what's wrong?

The trouble is that the d and the n in the first equation,

$d = n + 3$,

stand for the <u>numbers</u> of coins, but the d and the n in the second equation,

$d + n = 90$,

stand for the <u>total values</u> of the coins. Notice that the solver did not explain the variables clearly (Lesson 3).

<u>Correct solution</u>:

Think about the nature of a coin. Each dime Sue has is worth 10¢. We will choose our dime variable, d, to be Sue's <u>number</u> of dimes. Then 10¢ x d will be how much her dimes are worth.

Put d = the number of dimes Sue has.

Put n = the number of nickels Sue has.

Then $10d$ = how much (¢) Sue's dimes are worth.

And $5n$ = how much (¢) Sue's nickels are worth.

So we have

$d = n + 3$

$10d + 5n = 90$

EXAMPLE 5.4:

Tom has three more dimes than nickels. They total $1.35. How many dimes has Tom? How many nickels?

<u>Wrong solution</u>:

The unthinking person has learned from solving Example 5.3 above. But, still not thinking, (s)he writes,

Put d = the number of dimes Tom has.

Put n = the number of nickels Tom has.

Then $$d = n + 3$$

$$10d + 5n = \$1.35$$

Do you see what's wrong with the second equation? (The left side is in cents, but the right side is in dollars. We must either use cents for both sides or dollars for both sides.)

<u>Correct solution</u>:

Put d = the number dimes Tom has.

Put n = the number of nickels Tom has.

Then

$$d = n + 3$$
$$10d + 5n = 135$$ OR $$d = n + 3$$
$$.10d + .05n = 1.35$$

Some mixture problems are like coin problems.

EXAMPLE 5.5:

I want to mix two kinds of candy so that the total is 10 pounds at $3 a pound. The cheaper candy sells for $1.50 a pound. The other is $4 a pound. How much of each kind should be used?

Put c = the number of pounds to be used of the cheaper candy.

Put e = the number of pounds to be used of the more expensive candy.

Then $1.50c$ = the value ($) of the cheaper candy to be used.

And $4e$ = the value ($) of the more expensive candy to be used.

The mixture will weigh 10 pounds, so

$$c + e = 10.$$

And the mixture will sell for $3 a pound, so

$$1.50c + 4e = 10(3).$$

So we have

$$c + e = 10$$

$$1.50c + 4e = 10(3)$$

PRACTICE PROBLEMS FOR LESSON 5

Solve and check. Explain your variables.

1. The sum of the digits of a two-digit number is 11. When the digits are reversed, the new number is 27 less than the given number. What is the given number?

2. Arnie has dimes and nickels totaling $1.60. If he had four more dimes, he'd have twice as many dimes as he has nickels. How many dimes does he have? How many nickels?

3. Pecans sell for $3.50 a pound. Almonds sell for $5 a pound. How many pounds of each should be used to make 15 pounds of a mixture that sells for $4 a pound?

4. It took an hour for a boat to go six miles upstream. Using the same effort and taking the same path, the boat took only 45 minutes to return. What was the speed of the boat in still water? What was the speed of the current?

LESSON 6:

USE YOUR COMMON SENSE

Sometimes we have trouble with algebraic word problems because we don't know much about the subject the problem talks about. But before we give up on a problem, we should try using our common sense.

EXAMPLE 6.1:

Jones has one liter of a solution which, by volume, is 90% acid and 10% water. How much water should be added to make the solution 75% acid (by volume)?

> We don't have to know chemistry to solve this problem. The total mixture is 1 liter, and 90% of this, or .9 liter, is acid. We won't add any acid. So after we add the extra water, we'll still have .9 liter of acid.
>
> There are a couple of ways we can do this one. Here is one way:
>
> Put w = the volume of water (in liters) to be added.
>
> Then the total volume will be 1 + w liters, of which 75% will be acid. But the acid will still total .9 liter. So 75% of the total volume will equal .9 liter. So
>
> So, .75(1 + w) = .9
>
> Solving, we get w = .2. So we add .2 liter of water.
>
>
> Here is another way to do this problem:
>
> Put t = the total volume (in liters) of the mixture after the extra water has been added.
>
> Then 75% is acid. And the total acid is still .9 liter.
>
> So
>
> .75t = .9
>
> Solving, we get t = 1.2. The volume before adding the extra water was
>
> 1 liter, and the new volume is 1.2 liters. So the difference, .2 liter, is the amount of water added.

Mathematically, EXAMPLES 6.2 and 6.3 below are exactly the same as EXAMPLE 6.1.

EXAMPLE 6.2:

Smith has a pound of grass seed that is 90% Merion Bluegrass and 10% Kentucky Bluegrass by weight. How much Kentucky Bluegrass must be added in order to make the mixture 75% Merion Bluegrass by weight?

EXAMPLE 6.3:

Brown has roped off three equal parts of land. On one part, he planted 90% zinnias and 10% marigolds. How much of another part should be planted with marigolds in order to make the zinnias 75% of the total (of zinnias and marigolds)? (Assume that all seeds planted will grow.)

PRACTICE PROBLEMS FOR LESSON 6

Solve and check. Explain your variables.

1. A store owner has a pound of a mixture of nuts that is 90% peanuts and 10% Brazil nuts by weight. How much weight in Brazil nuts must be added to make the mixture 75% peanuts?

2. A law of physics says that a seesaw will be evenly balanced by two people (sitting on opposite sides of its center) when the product of one person's weight and his distance from the center equals the product of the other person's weight and his distance from the center. You are given a twelve-foot seesaw. Tell if it can be evenly balanced under each of these conditions. If so, tell how. If not, tell why not.

    a. Amy weighs 80 pounds and sits 3 feet from the center. Peter weighs 60 pounds.

    b. Paul and Ann each weigh 70 pounds.

    c. Perry weighs 50 pounds and sits at one end. Annette weighs 40 pounds.

3. A camera store owner makes a set profit on each roll of film she sells. Yesterday she sold a certain number of rolls of film. If she had sold 5 fewer but made 1¢ more on each, her profit on them would have been $2.80 less. If she had sold 10 more but made 1¢ less on each, her profit on them would have been $6.65 more. How many did she sell? What was the profit on each one? What was the total profit on them?

4. The formula to convert temperature from Celsius to Fahrenheit is $F = aC + b$, where F is the Fahrenheit temperature, C is the Celsius temperature, and where a and b are constants.

    a. Use the above information to figure out what a and b are and to write the given formula using your results, if 0° Celsius = 32° Fahrenheit, and if 100° Celsius = 212° Fahrenheit.

    b. The normal temperature of the human body is 98.6° Fahrenheit. What temperature is this in Celsius?

    c. A comfortable room temperature is 70° Fahrenheit. What temperature is this in Celsius?

LESSON 7:

IF ALL ELSE FAILS, TRY THE "WILD GUESS" METHOD

Now suppose you've tried everything we've talked about so far. And suppose you still can't figure out how to set up equations to solve a word problem. Then what? Then try the "wild guess" method.

The "wild guess" method works like this:

1. Take a wild guess at the answer. (You don't even have to guess close.)

2. Treat your guess as though it's really the answer. Check it out by seeing if it works in the problem, BUT DON'T DO ANYTHING IN YOUR HEAD. WRITE DOWN EVERYTHING YOU'RE FIGURING while you're checking it out.

3. When you're through checking out your guess, replace your guess with a variable.

4. Solve the resulting equation(s), and you'll get the real answer to the problem.

EXAMPLE 7.1:

Four years ago, Boris was half as old as he will be eight years from now. How old is Boris?

1. My wild guess is 35.

2. Four years ago, Boris was 35 – 4, or 31.

   Eight years from now, Boris will be 35 + 8, or 43.

   Now does 31 = $\frac{1}{2}$ of 43? No.

3. Put B = Boris's age (in years) now.

   Now replace 35 with B.

   Then four years ago, Boris was

   $B - 4$.

   Eight years from now he'll be

   $B + 8$.

   Now remember that "31 = 35 – 4" in step 2 is "$B - 4$" here.

   And remember that "43 = 35 + 8" in step 2 is "$B + 8$" here.

   So, instead of 31 = $\frac{1}{2}$ of 43, we have

   $B - 4 = \frac{1}{2}(B + 8)$.

4. Solving, we get

   $B = 16$.

So Boris's age is 16. Four years ago he was 12, and eight years from now he'll be 24. And 12 is half of 24. So 16 is the right answer.

EXAMPLE 7.2:

I want to mix two kinds of candy so that the total is 10 pounds at $3 a pound. One kind is $1.50 a pound. The other kind is $4 a pound. How much of each kind should be used in the mixture?

1. My wild guess is 7 pounds of the cheaper candy and 3 pounds of the more expensive candy.

2. The total is to be 10 pounds. Does 7 + 3 = 10? Yes.

    The cheaper candy is $1.50 a pound, so there will be $1.50(7) worth of this candy in the mixture.

    The other candy is $4 a pound, so there will be $4(3) worth of this candy in the mixture.

    The total will be 10 pounds at $3 a pound, or $30.

    So does $1.50(7) + $4(3) = $30? No.

3. Put c = the number of pounds of the cheaper candy to be used.

    Put e = the number of pounds of the more expensive candy to be used.

    Now replace each 7 with c, and replace each 3 with e.

    Then

    $c + e = 10$

    $1.5c + 4e = 30.$

4. Solving, we get

    $c = 4$

    $e = 6$

EXAMPLE 7.3:

It took an hour for a boat to go two kilometers upstream. Using the same effort, and taking the same path, it took 45 minutes to return. What was the speed of the boat in still water? What was the speed of the current?

1. My wild guess is 5 kph for the boat and 3 kph for the current.

2. Distance = rate x time.

    Upstream, the distance was 2 kilometers and the time was 1 hour.
    So 2 = rate x 1.

    The rate upstream was the boat's speed minus the current's speed.

    So does 2 = (5 – 3) x 1? Yes.

    Downstream, the distance was 2 kilometers and the time was 45 minutes,

    which is $\frac{3}{4}$ hour. So 2 = rate x $\frac{3}{4}$.

    The rate downstream was the boat's speed plus the current's speed.

    So does 2 = (5 + 3) x $\frac{3}{4}$? No.

3. Put b = the speed of the boat (kph) in still water.

    Put c = the speed of the current (kph).

    Now replace each 5 with b, and replace each 3 with c.

    Then

    $2 = (b - c)1$

    $2 = (b + c)\frac{3}{4}$

4. Solving, we get

    $b = 2\frac{1}{3}$

    $c = \frac{1}{3}$

PRACTICE PROBLEMS FOR LESSON 7

Try the "wild guess" method on some of the other problems in this book.

1. Do problem 5 in Lesson 3.

2. Do problem 6 in Lesson 3.

3. Do problem 8 in Lesson 3.

4. Do problem 1 in Lesson 5.

5. Do problem 2 in Lesson 5.

6. Do problem 3 in Lesson 5.

7. Do problem 4 in Lesson 5.

8. Do problem 1 in Lesson 6.

9. Do problem 3 in Lesson 6.

WARM UP

AGES

1. Let J = John's age (in years) now. How old was John a year ago?

2. Let A = Adelita's age (in months) now. How old was Adelita this month last year?

3. Let S = Samson's age (in years) now. How old was Samson six months ago?

4. Let B = Barton's age (in months) now. How old was Barton exactly two years ago?

5. Mrs. Ebbing is five years younger than her sister, whose age (in years) is s. How old is Mrs. Ebbing?

6. Mrs. Ebbing, whose age (in years) is E, is five years younger than her sister. How old is her sister?

7. Let F = Francine's age (in years). She is twice as old as her sister and ten years older than her brother. How old is her sister? Her brother?

8. Let *C* = Carlo's age (in years). How old will Carlo be eight months from now?

9. Brad was *B* years old last year. How old is he this year?

10. If Joe, who is *J* years old, were ten years younger, he would be the same age as his brother. How old is his brother?

11. If Joe, who is *J* years old, were ten years younger, he would be three years older than his sister. How old is his sister?

12. If Yolanda, who is *Y* years old, were only half as old, she would be three years younger than her brother. How old is her brother?

13. Let *B* = Bob's age (in years) now.

   a. In three years, Bob will be five years older than his sister will be. How old is his sister?

   b. In three years, Bob will be twice as old as his brother will be. How old is his brother?

   c. Bob's neighbor is ten years older than Bob will be next year. How old is Bob's neighbor?

14. Mr. and Mrs. Lee have three children, who are *A*, *B*, and *C* years old.

    a.   What is the total of the children's ages?

    b.   Mr. Lee is ten years older than twice the total of his children's ages. How old is Mr. Lee?

    c.   Mrs. Lee is five years older than her husband. How old is she?

15. Sandy, who is *S* years old, has a dog and a cat. The dog is three years older than the cat, who is eight years younger than Sandy. How old is the cat? The dog?

16. Mark is twice as old as Pedro and a third as old as Randy.

    a.   Let *M* = Mark's age. How old is Pedro? Randy?

    b.   Let *P* = Pedro's age. How old is Mark? Randy?

    c.   Let *R* = Randy's age. How old is Mark? Pedro?

17. If Kathy were five years older and Pauline were three years younger, they would be the same age. Kathy is *K* years old. How old is Pauline?

18. Let *A*, *B*, and *C* = the ages (in years) now of Alice, Bill, and Cheryl. Write an equation to show each statement made.

    a.   Alice is four years younger than Bill.

    b.   Five years from now, Bill will be twice as old as he was three years ago.

    c.   Cheryl is half as old as the combined ages of Alice and Bill.

    d.   The total of Alice's and Cheryl's ages is five years more than Bill's age.

    e.   If Bill were five years younger, he would be a year younger than Alice.

    f.   Cheryl is one and a half times as old as Bill was five years ago.

    g.   The total of Bill's and Cheryl's ages is one year less than three times Alice's age.

    h.   Cheryl will be twice as old (as she is now) in nine years.

i. If Bill were one year older, he would be the same age as Cheryl will be in three years.

j. If Bill were two years younger, he would be two years older than Alice.

k. The total of twice Bill's age and three times Cheryl's age is seven times Alice's age.

l. The total of twice Bill's age and three times Cheryl's age is the square of Alice's age.

m. When Cheryl is twice as old as she was four years ago, she will be one year younger than Bill is now.

n. If Bill were ten years younger and Alice were one year older, their combined ages would be Cheryl's age.

o. The square of Bill's age less the square of Cheryl's age is twice as much as the total of their ages.

p. The total of half of Alice's age and a third of Cheryl's age is one year more than half of Bill's age.

COINS

Let p = the number of pennies, n = the number of nickels, and so on. Assume all money is worth exactly its face value.

19. Jacob has an unknown number of nickels and quarters.

    a. How much are the nickels worth?

    b. How much are the quarters worth?

    c. How much do the coins total?

20. Jennifer has more nickels than pennies. What is the difference in their values?

21. Alberto has five more quarters than he has dimes. How much (total) does he have in terms of

    a. quarters?

    b. dimes?

22. Darlene has twice as many pennies as nickels. How much (total) does she have in terms of

    a. pennies?

    b. nickels?

23. Charles has twice as many quarters as dimes. How much (total) does he have in terms of

    a. dimes?

    b. quarters?

24. Ru-Mei has five fewer quarters than dimes. How much (total) does he have in terms of

    a. dimes?

    b. quarters?

25. Angelo has twice as many dimes as quarters, and five more nickels than dimes. How much (total) does he have in terms of

    a. nickels?

    b. dimes?

    c. quarters?

26. If Mary had five fewer pennies, she would have twice as many dimes as pennies. How much (total) does she have in terms of pennies?

27. Lila has some pennies, nickels, dimes, and quarters. Write an equation to show each statement made. (Not all of the statements can be true.)

    a.   If she had two fewer dimes and three fewer quarters, the dimes and the quarters would be worth the same amount.

    b.   The total of her quarters is 75¢ more than the total of her nickels.

    c.   The total of her nickels is 20¢ less than the total of her dimes.

    d.   If she had one more quarter, they would be worth three times as much as her nickels.

    e.   The total value of the pennies, nickels, and dimes is 3¢ more than the value of the quarters.

    f.   If she had five more nickels and two fewer dimes, their total value would equal the value of her quarters.

    g.   The total number of her pennies and dimes is the same as the total number of her nickels and quarters.

    h.   If she had one more quarter, their total value would be a dollar more than the total value of her nickels.

i. If she had seventeen more pennies and two fewer dimes, the total value of her pennies, nickels, and dimes would be the same as the value of her quarters.

j. If she had three times as many nickels and twice as many dimes, she would have $1.70 more than she has now.

k. The total value of her dimes and quarters is $1.45 more than the total value of her nickels.

l. If she had three more dimes, their total value would be twice as much as that of her nickels.

m. If she had double the number of nickels and dimes, she would have $1.15 more than she now has in quarters.

n. If she had five times the number of pennies and two fewer nickels, their total values would be equal.

o. If she gave away a nickel and then spent half of what she had left, she would have one cent less than her quarters now are worth.

p. Her dimes are worth 2¢ less than nine times her pennies.

MEASUREMENTS

Note: Let *f* = number of feet, *h* = number of hours, and so on.

28. Write a formula to show

    a.   the number of feet in *y* yards.

    b.   the number of minutes in *h* hours.

    c.   the number of days in *w* weeks.

    d.   the number of centimeters in *m* meters.

    e.   the number of hours in *d* days.

    f.   the number of feet in *m* miles.

    g.   the approximate number of weeks in *y* years.

    h.   the number of seconds in *h* hours.

    i.   the number of miles a car travels at *s* miles an hour in *h* hours.

    j.   the number of ounces in *p* pounds.

29. A room is three feet longer than it is wide. What is its area in terms of its

  a. width?

  b. length?

30. Write a formula to show

  a. distance in terms of rate and time.

  b. rate in terms of distance and time.

  c. time in terms of distance and rate.

31. Mrs. Loring drove for *h* hours. Write an expression to show how long she would have driven if she had driven for

  a. two hours less.

  b. five hours more.

  c. half an hour more.

  d. fifteen minutes less.

  e. twenty-three minutes more.

32. Mr. Brown drove for *h* hours at *k* kilometers an hour. He would have arrived at his destination three hours earlier if he had gone twenty kilometers an hour faster. Write a formula to express this.

33. If a bicyclist had gone five miles an hour faster, she would have arrived at her destination 10 minutes earlier. Write a formula to show this.

34. A canoeist is paddling at *p* kph. The river is flowing at *c* kph. How many kph is the canoe traveling if it is going

    a. against the current?

    b. with the current?

35. A canoe travels downriver (with the current) at *r* mph. How fast would it be going in still water?

36. An airplane would travel at a speed of *s* kph in still air. But there is an air current of *c* kph. How fast does the plane travel if it is going in

    a. the same direction as the air current?

    b. the opposite direction of the air current?

37. A clock runs three minutes slow each day. Suppose it starts off showing the correct time.

    a. How much would it be off after *d* days?

    b. How long would it be before it showed the correct time again?

38. A room is *w* feet wide and *l* feet long. What would its area be (in square feet) if

    a. the width were two feet less?

    b. the length were three feet more?

    c. the width were two feet less and the length were four feet more?

    d. the width were six inches more?

    e. the length were seven inches less?

39. Swiss cheese is *p* dollars for half a pound. How much will

    a. two pounds cost?

    b. one pound six ounces cost?

40. A bird is flying at the rate of *b* kph directly toward a train. The train is traveling at *t* kph.

   a. How fast are they approaching each other?

   b. How long will it be before they meet?

41. There are 32 ounces in a quart of milk. How many glasses, each holding *g* ounces, can be filled by

   a. *q* quarts of milk?

   b. *h* half-gallons of milk?

42. A nursery school uses *q* quarts of milk each weekday. How many gallons of milk does it use

   a. each weekday?

   b. in a (five-day) week?

43. A car went for h_1 hours at m_1 mph, and then it went for h_2 hours at m_2 mph. How far

   a. did it go all together?

   b. would it have gone if m_1 had been 3 mph faster?

44. Carpeting is sold by the square yard. A room is *w* feet wide and *l* feet long. How much will it cost to carpet the room if the carpeting costs $16.25 (square) yard?

45. One side of a cube is *s* feet long. What would be its volume

    a.   in cubic feet?

    b.   in cubic inches?

    c.   in cubic feet, if each side were two feet shorter?

    d.   in cubic inches, if each side were two feet shorter?

    e.   in cubic feet, if each side were one inch shorter?

    f.   in cubic inches, if each side were one inch shorter?

46. The area of a circle is πr^2, where *r* is in feet. What will the area be in square feet if the circle's diameter is

    a.   increased by two feet?

    b.   decreased by six inches?

    c.   decreased by seven inches?

NUMBERS

Note: Let u = the units' digit, t = the tens' digit, and h = the hundreds' digit if the problem is about a two- or three-digit number. Let n = the numerator and d the denominator of a fraction.

47. Jane is thinking of a two-digit number. Write an expression to show

    a.   the number Jane is thinking of.

    b.   three more than the number Jane is thinking of.

    c   fifteen more than the number Jane is thinking of.

    d.   a number whose digits are in the reverse order of those in Jane's number.

    e.   the sum of the digits in Jane's number.

    f.   the product of the digits in Jane's number.

    g.   a number that is twice as much as Jane's number.

    h.   a number that is five less than half of Jane's number.

48. Joe is thinking of a three-digit number. Write an expression to show

    a.   the number Joe is thinking of.

    b.   a number whose digits are in the reverse order of Joe's number.

    c.   a number that is twice as much as Joe's number.

    d.   the sum of the numbers in answers a and b above.

    e.   the difference between the numbers in answers a and b above.

    f–g.   the positive difference between the numbers in answers a and b above if in Joe's number

        f.   the hundreds' digit is greater than the units' digit.

        g.   the hundreds' digit is less than the units' digit.

    h.   a number that is 500 more than Joe's number.

    i.   a number that is one more than three times Joe's number.

49. Observe the answers to items e-g in problem 48. Suppose someone tells you to write a three-digit number and then to write the number with the digits reversed and then to subtract the smaller number from the larger one. What numbers must be factors of the final result? (Try it a few times to convince yourself it really works.)

50. Isaac is thinking of a fraction. Write an expression to show

    a. the fraction Isaac is thinking of.

    b. a fraction whose numerator is two more than Isaac's.

    c. the reciprocal of Isaac's fraction.

    d. the sum of Isaac's fraction and its reciprocal.

    e. a fraction whose numerator is three less and whose denominator is five more than Isaac's fraction.

    f. a number that is six more than the number in e above.

    g. three times the sum of Isaac's fraction and its reciprocal.

WORK RATES

Note: Use meaningful variables. For example, if a problem talks about Paul and Edward, use P and E for the variables. Assume that if two people work on a job together, their overall work rate is the sum of their individual work rates.

51. Pamela can do a job in P hours, and Rachel can do the job in R hours. Write an expression to show how much of the job can be done

    a.   by Pamela in one hour.

    b.   by Rachel in one hour.

    c.   in one hour if the two people work on it together.

    d.   by Pamela in h hours.

    e.   in h hours if the two people work on it together.

    f.   in h hours if Pamela works on it continuously but Rachel waits two hours before she starts helping.

    g.   in h hours if Pamela works on it only the first two and the last two hours and Rachel works on it the rest of the time.

52. Pipe A can fill a water tank in *A* minutes. Pipe B can fill it in *B* minutes. Pipe C can empty it in *C* minutes. Write an expression to show how much of the tank will be filled if the valves of pipes

    a.   A and B are open, and C is closed, for *m* minutes.

    b.   A and C are open, and B is closed, for *m* minutes.

    c.   A, B, and *C* are open for *m* minutes.

    d.   B and C are closed, but A is open for ten minutes, after which all three valves are open for *m* minutes.

    e.   A and C are closed and B is partially opened for *m* minutes, during which the flow through pipe B is two-thirds of its normal rate.

    f.   A and C are open, and B is closed, for ten minutes, after which A and B are open and C is closed. The total time (including the first ten minutes) is *m* minutes.

    g.   A is open. Eight minutes later, B is opened, and seven minutes after that, C is opened. All three valves are closed *m* minutes after valve C was opened.

MIXTURES

53. A chemist has *c* centiliters of an 85% alcohol solution.

   a–d.   Write an expression to show how much pure alcohol she

   a. has now.

   b. will have if she adds *c* centiliters of another 85% alcohol solution to it.

   c. will have if she adds *c* centiliters of a 70% alcohol solution to it.

   d. will have if she adds *c* centiliters of water to it.

   e–h.   Tell how much solution and what concentration of alcohol she will have if she adds to it

   e. *c* centiliters of another 85% alcohol solution.

   f. *c* centiliters of a 70% alcohol solution.

   g. *c* centiliters of water.

   h. *d* centiliters of water.

54. A grocer has ten pounds of a coffee blend that is 80% Columbian coffee. How much coffee, and what will be the percent of Columbian coffee in it, will he have if he adds to the ten pounds

  a. ten pounds of coffee that is 70% Columbian?

  b. fifteen pounds of coffee that is 80% Columbian?

  c. fifteen pounds of coffee that is 60% Columbian?

  d. ten pounds of coffee that is 0% Columbian?

  e. p pounds of coffee that is 80% Columbian?

  f. p pounds of coffee that is 0% Columbian?

  g. p pounds of coffee that is 70% Columbian?

  h. ten pounds of coffee that is 70% Columbian and ten pounds of coffee that is 60% Columbian?

  i. p pounds of coffee that is 70% Columbian and q pounds of coffee that is 60% Columbian and r pounds of coffee that is 30% Columbian?

55. A party store sells mixed nuts for $4 a pound and peanuts for $2.50 a pound.

   a-b.   Write an expression to show the total selling price of

      a.   three pounds of mixed nuts and *p* pounds of peanuts.

      b.   *m* pounds of mixed nuts and *p* pounds of peanuts.

   c-e.   Write an equation to show the average selling price, *a*, of

      c.   three pounds of mixed nuts and *p* pounds of peanuts.

      d.   *m* pounds of mixed nuts and *p* pounds of peanuts.

      e.   ten pounds of nuts if *m* pounds were mixed nuts and the rest were peanuts.

   f-h.   Write an equation that, when solved, will determine how many pounds of each should be used to make

      f.   ten pounds of a mixture selling for $3 a pound.

      g.   *t* pounds of a mixture selling for $3 a pound.

      h.   *t* pounds of a mixture selling for $*d* a pound.

INTEREST

56. Mr. Wendel invested $5,000 at r% annual interest and $3,000 at b% annual interest. What is his annual income from these two investments?

57. Ms. Bender earns r% annual interest on an investment. What is the quarterly rate of interest earned?

58. Ms. Zender earns 6% annual interest on an investment of $$d$, and r% annual interest on an investment of $2,000.

    a. What is her annual income from these investments?

    b. Suppose she could collect her income from these investments quarterly. How much would this quarterly income be?

59. Mr. Martinez has a total of $10,000 invested. Some is at an annual rate of r%, and the rest is at an annual rate of b%. How much is his annual income from these investments if

    a. $6,000 is invested at r%?

    b. $$s$ is invested at r%?

$A = P(1+ r)^n$ shows the amount accumulated, A, by an investment of P dollars at a periodic rate of interest, r, compounded for n periods. Use this formula for problems 60–63.

60. a–d.   If the rate is 9% annually, what figure should be used for r if the interest is compounded

        a. annually?

        b. semiannually?

        c. quarterly?

        d. monthly?

    e–h.   Suppose the principal invested (P) is left to accumulate for three years. What figure should be used for n if the interest is compounded

        e. annually?

        f. semiannually?

        g. quarterly?

        h. monthly?

61. Write a formula to show how much an investment of $2,000 is worth at the end of

    a.   two years at 8% compounded annually.

    b.   two years at 8% compounded quarterly.

    c.   five years at 6% compounded annually.

    d.   five years at 6% compounded monthly.

62. Write an equation to show how much would have to be invested in order to have

    a. $5,000 at the end of five years of 8% annual interest compounded quarterly.

    b. $7,450.85 at the end of eight years of 10% annual interest compounded semiannually.

63. A credit card company charges 1.5% a month on the unpaid balance. Write a formula to show how much will be owed on an original balance of $500 if no payments are made for

    a.   two months

    b.   one year

MISCELLANEOUS

64. Judith works at an hourly rate of pay, *r*. Write a formula to show how much her gross pay, *G*, is for *h* hours if

    a. all hours are paid at straight time.

    b. the first forty hours are paid at straight time and all hours over forty are paid at time and a half.

    c. she is to get forty hours at straight time, ten hours at time and a half, and five hours at double time.

    d. thirty hours are to be paid at straight time, *t* hours at time and a half, and all other hours at double time.

65. Jeff's average monthly salary for the first six months of the year was *f* and for the last six months of the year was *g*. Write an expression to show his average monthly salary for the whole year.

66. Nora's average monthly salary for the first three months of the year was *f*, for the next three months was *g*, for the next two months was *h*, and for the last four months was *k*. Write an expression to show her average monthly salary for the year.

67.   Mr. Summers bought a suit discounted 25% from its regular price of *s* and a pair of slacks discounted 30% from their regular price of *k*. What total did the two items cost him?

68.   Lara's average score for five tests was *a*. What will

   a.   her average score be if she scores *n* on her next test?

   b.   she need to score on the next test in order to bring her average score to *b*? (Hint: Let *b* = your answer to part a above, and solve the equation for *n*.)

69.   A total of $*t* was collected from *p* people, who each contributed $*c*.

   a.   Write an equation to show the total collected.

   b.   The total would have been the same if five fewer people had contributed but each one had given $3 more. Write an equation to show the total collected.

70.   Ms. Alston had 7% of her gross pay withheld for social security tax, 23% for federal income tax, and 5% for state income tax. Her net pay was *N*. How much was her gross pay?

71.   What equation says that the product of *d* and *c* is the same as the product of three less than *d* and five more than *c*?

© 2001 Critical Thinking Books & Software • www.criticalthinking.com • 800-458-4849

AGES

Instructions:

     a.   Show your work.

     b.   Give your answers in years.

1. Ten years more than three times Charlie's age is two years less than five times his age. How old is he?

2. When Alice is three times as old as she was five years ago, she will be twice her present age. How old is she?

3. The sum of Gary's and Vivian's ages is twenty-three years. Gary is seven years older than Vivian. How old is each person?

4. Brad is five years younger than Louise. The sum of their ages is thirty-one years. How old is each person?

5. The sum of the ages of Juan and Herman is twenty-four years. Juan is twice as old as Herman. How old is each one?

6. If Edith were five years older, she would be twice Fred's age. If she were three years younger, she would be exactly his age. How old is each one?

7. When Leonard is five years older than double his present age, he will be three times as old as he was a year ago. How old is he?

8. If Karen were two years older than she is, she would be twice as old as Larry, who is eight years younger than she. How old is each one?

9. Edmund is three years older than Frank. The sum of their ages is nineteen years. How old is each one?

10. Helen's and Ivan's ages total eighteen years. Helen is two years younger than Ivan. How old are they?

11. Mortimer was born six years before Petunia. The sum of their ages is twenty-eight years. How old are they?

12. When Davi is twice as old as he was two years ago, he will be three times as old as he was five years ago. How old is he now?

13. Jeff is twice as old as Amos was three years ago. The sum of their ages is thirty-nine years. How old is each one now?

14. When Sandy's age is three years more than twice as much as it was five years ago, he will be fourteen years older than he is now. How old is he?

15. If John were three times as old as he is, he would be twice as old as his sister is. His sister is five years older than he. How old is each one?

16. Nine years ago, Phyllis was four times as old as Edwina. If Phyllis were five years older than she is now, she would be twice as old as Edwina is now. How old is each girl?

17. Three times Andy's age is eleven more than twice Belinda's age. The sum of their ages is two less than twice Belinda's age. How old is each person?

18. Joe is ten years older than Mary was two years ago, at which time Joe was twice as old as Mary. How old is each one now?

19. In two years, Winston, who is eight years older than Xavier, will be twice as old as Xavier. How old is each now?

20. The difference between Alan's and Bea's ages is three years. The sum of their ages is twenty-seven years. How old are they if

    a. Alan is older than Bea?

    b. Bea is older than Alan?

21. When Karl is seventeen, he will be five years older than Laura was when she was twice as old as Karl is now. How old is Karl?

22. Martin and Natalie would be the same age if Martin were two years older and Natalie were three years younger. The sum of their ages is twenty-nine years. How old is each?

23. Three times Blake's age subtracted from five times Amanda's age is Blake's age. The sum of their ages is twenty-seven years. How old is each?

24. When Ms. Morley was three times as old as Jennie, they were seven years younger than they are now. Now Ms. Morley is twice as old as Jennie. How old are they?

25. Nelson is twice as old as Charles was four years ago. The sum of their ages now is thirty-four years. How old is each?

26. If Stella were five years older, she would be twice as old as Ted, who is three years younger than she. How old is each one?

27. The sum of the ages of Carl and Daria is twice as much as the difference between their ages. How old is Daria if Carl is nine years old and is

    a.   older than she?

    b.   younger than she?

28. The sum of the ages of Don and his brother is twenty-four years. The difference is ten years. How old are they?

29. A plaid elephant is two years older than a striped leopard named Leo, who is five times as old as a polka-dotted zebra. A year from now the elephant will still be two years older than the leopard (you already knew that, didn't you?), but the leopard will be only four times as old as the zebra will be. How old is each one now?

30. Yancy is two years older than Zelda, who is four years older than Alice. The sum of their ages is twenty-two years. How old is each person?

31. If Barbara were twice as old as Carla, who is four years older than Dorothy, the sum of all three ages would be forty-eight years. How old is

    a. Carla?

    b. Dorothy?

32. If Carole were five years older and Marty were five years younger, then Carole would be twice as old as Marty. If Marty were five years older and Carole were five years younger, then Marty's age would be three times Carole's age. How old is each one?

33. Twice Edmund's age is half of Franklin's age. How old is

    a. Edmund, if Franklin is twelve?

    b. Franklin, if Edmund is two and a half?

34. In five years, Henry will be twice as old as his brother will be. His brother is eight years younger than he. How old is each one?

35. If Christine were five years older, she would be twice as old as Donna is. If Donna were five years older, she would be three times as old as Christine is. How old is each one?

36. Eduardo's aunt is three times as old as he is. She is twice as old as his brother. Eduardo is five years younger than his brother. What are the ages of the three people?

37. Next year Peter will be twice as old as his sister will be. She is three years younger than he. How old is each one now?

38. In three years, Margaret will be four years more than twice as old as Nancy will be. Nancy is eight years younger than Margaret. How old is each one now?

39. Five years ago, Uhle was three times as old as Valerie was. Next year he will be twice as old as she will be. How old is each one now?

40. Mrs. Markham is five years younger than her husband, who is three times as old as their son Jim. The sum of all three ages is one hundred seven years. How old is

    a. Jim?

    b. Mr. Markham?

    c. Mrs. Markham?

41. Joe is twice as old as Hank was two years ago. Hank is three times as old as Yvonne, who is six years younger than Joe. How old is

    a. Joe?

    b. Hank?

    c. Yvonne?

42. Andy is half as old as he will be in five years. How old is he?

43. Two years ago, Betty was half as old as she will be in four years. How old is she now?

44. Next year Francesca will be half as old as she will be in ten years. How old is she now?

45. If Randall were seven years older, he would be half as old as his mother, who is two years older than four times Randall's age. How old is each one?

46. Last year Paula was one-third as old as Richard was. Next year she will be half the age that Richard will be. How old is each one now?

47. Half of Danielle's age is five years less than her age three years ago. How old is she?

48. In seven years, Tony will be twice as old as Brad will be. Brad is one-third Tony's age now. How old is each one?

49. When Scott was one-third as old as he will be in five years, he was half his present age. How old is he?

50. When Luke is twenty years older than he was when he was half his present age, he will be two and a half times as old as he is now. How old is he?

51. When Quincy was half as old as he is now, he was twice as old as his sister is now. His sister is twelve years younger than he. How old is each one now?

52. Two years ago, Jim was half as old as Eileen was. The sum of their ages now is twenty-eight years. How old is each one?

53. Darrell is half as old as he will be when he is three times as old as he was four years ago. How old is he?

54. When Wilma is half as old as she will be when she is three times as old as she is now, she will be twice as old as she was four years ago. How old is she?

55. When Julie was half as old as she will be five years from now, she was three times as old as Edward was last year. The sum of Julie's and Edward's ages next year will be twenty-six years. How old is each one now?

56. A year ago Greta was one-third as old as Hans was. Hans will be twice as old as Greta in another three years. How old is each now?

57. When Gerry was one-third as old as she is now, she was half as old as she was last year. How old is she now?

58. Two years ago Kathy was a third as old as she will be when she is twice as old as she is now. How old is she?

59. When Mark was eight years younger than he will be when he is three times as old as he is now, he will be twice as old as he was a year ago. How old is he?

60. Louise is two years older than Henry, who is seven years older than Marie, who is one-fourth as old as Louise. How old is

    a. Louise?

    b. Henry?

    c. Marie?

61. The sum of the ages of Donna and her two sisters is twenty-six years. Donna is twice as old as one of her sisters and is one and one-half times as old as the other. How old is each girl?

62. If Elwood's age is subtracted from the sum of the ages of Chester and Darla, the result is three years more than twice Darla's age. If Darla's age is subtracted from the sum of the ages of Chester and Elwood, the result is seven years less than twice Chester's age.

a. How old is Darla?

b. Who is the older of Chester and Elwood, and by how much?

63. Kiran is twice as old as she was when she was three years older than one-fifth of her present age. How old is she?

64. When Ernestine was half as old as she will be in two years, she was three years older than she was when she was only one-third as old as she is now. How old is she?

65. Brenda's age is twice Edna's age and one and a half times Gerard's age. The sum of their ages is twenty-six years. How old is each one?

COINS

Instructions:

    a.   Show your work.

    b.   If a problem asks for a money answer, show your answer in cents if it is less than a dollar. Show it in dollars if it is a dollar or more.

    c.   Assume that all information needed to solve a problem is given. For example, if a problem talks only about Bill's dimes and then asks how much money Bill has, assume that Bill has no money except the dimes.

66. Alex has fifteen nickels and dimes. He has seven more nickels than dimes.

    a.   How many of each kind of coin has he?

    b.   What is the total value of his coins?

67. Joel has two fewer quarters than dimes and a total of fourteen dimes and quarters.

    a.   How many of each kind of coin has he?

    b.   How much money has he?

68. Amalita has a total of seventeen nickels and dimes. How many of each does she have if they total

    a. $1.45?

    b.   90¢?

69. Antoinette has ninety-seven nickels and dimes totaling $7.10. How many of each kind of coin has she?

70. Belinda has twice as many nickels as dimes. How many of each does she have if they total

    a.   80¢?

    b. $1.20?

71. Angelo has twice as many dimes as quarters. If he had five fewer dimes and seven more quarters, he would have the same number of each.

    a.   How many of each kind of coin has he?

    b.   How much money has he?

72. Suppose you have seven more nickels than dimes. How many of each kind of coin do you have if they total

  a. 80¢?

  b. 65¢?

  c. $1.40?

73. Jan has $5 in nickels and dimes. How many of each kind of coin has she if

  a. she has ten more nickels than dimes?

  b. she has eight more dimes than nickels?

  c. the nickels total four times as much money as the dimes?

  d. the dimes total four times as much money as the nickels?

  e. she has twice as many nickels as dimes?

  f. she has twice as many dimes as nickels?

74. Yolanda has a total of thirty-seven nickels and dimes. The dimes come to 40¢ more than the nickels.

    a.   How many of each does she have?

    b.   How much money does she have?

75. Sue has a total of forty nickels and dimes. If she had eleven more coins, she would have 90¢ more. She now has two more dimes than nickels.

    a.   How many more each of nickels and dimes does she need to make the additional 90¢?

    b.   How many each of nickels and dimes does she have?

    c.   How much money does she have?

d–e. If she had the additional eleven coins,

    d.   how many of each kind would she have (total)?

    e.   how much money would she have (total)?

76. Lisa has a total of fifty-four nickels and dimes. If she had three more nickels, the face value of the coins would be $4. How many of each does she have?

77. If Bennett had a certain number more nickels and fewer dimes, he would have 60¢ less. What is the number?

78. Amy has two more nickels than dimes and five more dimes than quarters. Her nickels, dimes, and quarters total $3.25. How many of each kind of coin has she?

79. Luke has three times as many nickels as dimes and five times as many pennies as nickels.

    a–b. Suppose he has a total of thirty-eight coins. Then

        a.   how many of each kind of coin has he?

        b.   how much money has he?

        c.   Suppose he has $2.80. Then how many of each kind of coin has he?

80. If Kent had five fewer nickels and two fewer dimes, he would have the same number of nickels, dimes, and quarters.

      a. If he has a total of $12.85, how many of each kind of coin does he have?

    b–c. If he has one hundred fifty-one coins,

      b. how many of each kind does he have?

      c. how much money does he have?

81. Craig and Dennis each have some nickels and dimes. They both have the same amount of money, but Craig has four more nickels than Dennis has.

      a. What conclusion about dimes necessarily follows?

      b. Craig has fifty-seven coins. How many coins does Dennis have?

    c–d. If the boys pool their money, they will have $8.70. How many of each kind of coin does

      c. Craig have?

      d. Dennis have?

82. Linda's quarters total 75¢ more than her nickels total. Her nickels total 20¢ less than her dimes total. If she had one more quarter, they would be worth three times as much as her nickels.

    a. How many of each kind of coin has she?

    b. How much do they total?

83. Brenda has three nickels and a total of ten dimes and quarters. If she had three fewer quarters and two fewer dimes, she would have only half as much money. How many dimes and quarters has she?

84. A bank teller had one hundred thirty-five quarters, dimes, and nickels in his till totaling $23.50. There were three times as many quarters as nickels.

    a. How many nickels were there? How much did they total?

    b. How many dimes were there? How much did they total?

    c. How many quarters were there? How much did they total?

85. Lucille has dimes and quarters totaling $2.25. If the numbers of coins she has were reversed (if the number of dimes were instead the number of quarters, and vice versa), she would have 30¢ less. How many of each kind of coin does she have?

86. Dave's nickels and dimes total $1.55. His quarters and dimes total $4.25. His nickels and quarters total $3.80.

    a. How many of each kind of coin has he?

    b. How much money does he have?

87. Miranda has $5 more in dimes than in nickels but only two-thirds as many dimes as nickels.

    a. How many of each kind of coin does she have?

    b. How much money does she have?

88. Harry has twice as many dimes as quarters and one-third as many nickels as quarters. The total value of these coins is $4.20. How many of each kind has he?

89. Zeke has $10.20 in nickels, dimes, and quarters. He has twice as many quarters as dimes and four more dimes than nickels. How many of each kind of coin has he?

90. Fortunata has pennies, nickels, and dimes. How many of each kind has she if they total

    a. $1.17, and there are four times as many dimes as pennies and five more nickels than pennies?

    b. 97¢, and there is one more dime than pennies and five fewer nickels than pennies?

    c. $2.40, and there are the same number of each kind of coin?

    d. $3.60, and there are twice as many pennies as nickels and twice as many nickels as dimes?

    e. $1.93, and there is one-half less dime than half the total number of coins in nickels and pennies, and there are half as many nickels as pennies?

91. Bill has four more dimes than nickels, and seven fewer nickels than pennies. He has a total of $3.35. How many of each kind of coin has he?

92. Ken has twice as many quarters as dimes and half as many dimes as nickels. He has $3.50 total. How many of each kind of coin has he?

93. Yasmin's quarters total $2.80 more than her nickels, of which she has half as many as she has dimes, which total 80¢ more than her quarters.

   a. How many of each kind of coin has she?

   b. How much does each kind of coin total?

   c. How much money does Yasmin have?

94. Lavinia has eighteen more coins in nickels and dimes than she has in quarters and pennies. She has three times as many pennies as quarters and the same number of nickels as dimes. She has $4.25. How many of each kind of coin has she?

95. If Michelle had had twice as much as she had before she spent a third of her money, she would have $2.50 left. She started with a total of nine dimes and quarters.

    a. How much money did she start with?

    b. How much did she spend?

    c. How many of each kind of coin did she start with?

96. If Dominic had five more nickels and had twice as many dimes as that, he would have $3.05 more than he has. He has three more dimes than nickels.

    a. How many of each kind of coin has he?

    b. How much money has he?

97. Horace has nickels, dimes, and quarters totalling $4.85. If the numbers of nickels and dimes were reversed (if the number of nickels were instead the number of dimes, and vice versa), he would have $4.55. He has three more quarters than he has dimes. How many of each kind of coin does he have?

98. Kathy spent the morning collecting money for a charity. When she counted up the pennies, nickels, dimes, and quarters she had collected, the total was $89.38. There were five more quarters than dimes, twice as many dimes as nickels, and seventy-three more pennies than nickels. How many of each kind of coin did she collect?

99. If Eustace had twice as many nickels and half as many quarters, he would have 60¢ less. Suppose he now has

a–b. a total of sixteen nickels and quarters.

    a. How many of each kind of coin has he?

    b. How much money does he have?

    c. $1.65. How many of each kind of coin does he have?

100. If Norma had half again as many quarters as she has, and only one-third as many dimes as she has, she would have the same total number of coins but would have $3 more.

    a. How many of each kind of coin has she?

    b. How much money has she?

101. Laurence has some pennies, nickels, and dimes. How many of each kind has he, and how much do they total, if the total number of coins is

   a. fifteen, and there are two more dimes than nickels and two more nickels than pennies?

   b. one hundred twenty-five, and there are one-fourth as many dimes as the sum of the numbers of nickels and pennies, and there is one less nickel than one-eighth the sum of the numbers of pennies and dimes?

   c. fifty-six, and there are one-fifth as many dimes as nickels and two and a half times as many nickels as pennies?

   d. seventy-six, and there are one-eighth as many nickels and pennies and four fewer dimes than nickels?

   e. thirty, and there are twice as many nickels as dimes and two-thirds as many nickels as pennies?

102. If Theresa had half again as many dimes as she has, and only one-third as many quarters as she has, she would have three more coins but would have the same amount of money.

     a.   How many of each kind of coin has she?

     b.   How much money has she?

   c–d.   Suppose you are given the same information, except that Theresa would have six more, instead of three more, coins. Then

     c.   how many of each kind of coin has she?

     d.   how much money has she?

   e–g.   Suppose you are given the starting information, except that Theresa would have x more, instead of three more, coins. Then

     e.   how many of each kind of coin has she?

     f.   how much money has she?

     g.   what must be true of x in order for the problem to make sense in the real world?

MIXTURES

Note: Don't be alarmed if your answers don't come out to whole numbers. These are real-life problems, and in real life the answers to problems often contain fractions.

1. A chemist has one liter of a solution that is 90% acetic acid. How much water must be added to make the resulting solution 45% acetic acid?

2. A chemist has four liters of a solution that is 75% acetic acid. How much water must be added to make the resulting solution 60% acetic acid?

3. A chemist has one liter of a solution that is 75% acetic acid. How much water must be added to make the resulting solution 60% acetic acid?

4. A chemist has one liter of a solution that is 60% acetic acid. How much acetic acid must be added to make the resulting solution 75% acetic acid?

5. A feed store has one thousand pounds of a mixture that is 90% oats. How many pounds of other ingredients must be added to make the mixture 80% oats?

6. A feed store has three hundred pounds of a mixture that is 80% oats. How many pounds of oats must be added to make the mixture 90% oats?

7. Mr. Ling has five pounds of nuts that sell for $3.00 a pound. How many pounds of nuts that sell for $4.00 a pound must be added to have a mixture that sells for $3.50 a pound?

8. A mixture of 10% honey and 90% water is to be used as a sweetener.

    a. How much water should be added to a liter of honey?

    b. How much honey should be added to a liter of water?

9. A certain hair dye uses 5% active ingredients and 95% inactive ingredients. How much of

    a. inactive ingredients must be added to two liters of active ingredients?

    b. active ingredients must be added to two liters of inactive ingredients?

10. How much water must be added to a liter of alcohol to make the resulting mixture 80% alcohol?

11. How much water must be added to a liter of 80% alcohol to make the resulting mixture 70% alcohol?

12. How many pounds of jelly beans selling for $2.00 a pound should be added to four pounds of mixed candies selling for $2.75 a pound to produce a mixture selling for

    a. $2.25 a pound?

    b. $2.50 a pound?

13. A chemist has two liters of 70% sulfuric acid.

   a-c. How much sulfuric acid should be added to make a solution that is

        a.   75% sulfuric acid?

        b.   80% sulfuric acid?

        c.   90% sulfuric acid?

   d-f. How much water should be added to make a solution that is

        d.   65% sulfuric acid?

        e.   60% sulfuric acid?

        f.   50% sulfuric acid?

14. A butcher grinds up fifteen pounds of chuck steak to make hamburger. The chuck steak is 10% fat. How much suet may be legally added if the law allows hamburger to have

        a.   26% fat content?

        b.   20% fat content?

15. A pint of unhomogenized half-and-half is half cream and half skim milk.

a-b. Enough skim milk is added to make the mixture only 25% cream.

   a. How much skim milk is added?

   b. What will be the total quantity after the addition?

c-d. Enough cream is taken out to make the mixture only 25% cream.

   c. How much cream is taken out?

   d. What will be the quantity left afterwards?

e-f. Enough skim milk is taken out to make the mixture 75% cream.

   e. How much skim milk is taken out?

   f. What will be the quantity left afterwards?

g-h. Enough cream is added to make the mixture 75% cream.

   g. How much cream is added?

   h. What will be the quantity after the addition?

16. A pharmacist has a two-liter bottle of cough syrup mixture that is 90% water, 10% active ingredients.

    a–b. She adds enough water to make the mixture 95% water.

        a. How much water is added?

        b. What quantity will she have after the addition?

    c–d. She adds enough active ingredients to make the mixture contain only 85% water.

        c. How much of the active ingredients are added?

        d. What quantity will she have after the addition?

17. A candy store sells one kind of candy for $2.50 a pound and another kind for $3.50 a pound. How much of each kind should be used to make ten pounds of a mixture selling for

    a. $3.00 a pound?

    b. $2.75 a pound?

    c. $3.25 a pound?

18. Tom has eight grams of A and sixteen grams of B.

   a–b.   How much of A must be set aside to make a total weight that is

        a.   25% A?

        b.   90% B?

   c–d.   How much of B must be set aside to make a total weight that is

        c.   25% B?

        d.   90% A?

19. Ms. Black wants to use two kinds of candy to make fifteen pounds of a mixture that sells for $4.25 a pound. One kind of candy sells for $5.50 a pound and the other kind sells for $3.00 a pound. How many pounds of each should she use?

20. Two kinds of nuts are to be used to make ten pounds of a mixture that sells for $3.50 a pound. One kind of nut sells for $2.50 a pound and the other kind sells for $5.00 a pound. How many pounds of each must be used?

21. Brazilian coffee sells for $4 a pound. Columbian coffee sells for $9 a pound. How much of each kind should be used to make twenty pounds of a blend of the two that sells for

    a. $5 a pound?

    b. $6.50 a pound?

    c. $8 a pound?

22. How many pounds of 70% Columbian coffee must be added to ten pounds of 90% Columbian coffee to have

    a. 75% Columbian coffee?

    b. 80% Columbian coffee?

    c. 85% Columbian coffee?

    d. 82% Columbian coffee?

    e. p% Columbian coffee?

23. A party store sells mixed nuts for $5 a pound and peanuts for $2 a pound. In order to offer a cheaper mixture to the customers, the owner decides to include more peanuts.

   a–b. How many pounds of peanuts should be added to ten pounds of mixed nuts if the result is to sell for

      a. $4 a pound?

      b. $3 a pound?

   c–d. How many pounds of each should be used to have a total of ten pounds selling for

      c. $4 a pound?

      d. $3 a pound?

24. How much galena containing 5% lead should be combined with how much galena containing 17% lead to have five tons (10,000 pounds) of galena containing

   a. 8% lead?

   b. 12 1/2% lead?

25. Merion bluegrass seed sells for $8.00 a pound. Kentucky bluegrass seed sells for
     $6.50 a pound. How much of each should be used to make a mixture weighing

     a.   ten pounds and selling for $7.00 a pound?

     b.   fifteen pounds and selling for $7.25 a pound?

     c.   eight pounds and selling for $7.50 a pound?

26. For each answer to problem 25 that contains a fractional part of a pound,
     convert your answer to pounds and ounces.

27. Bologna sells for $1.50 a pound. Salami sells for $2.50 a pound. How much of
     each should be used to have ten pounds of a mixture of both selling for

     a. $1.75 a pound?

     b. $2.00 a pound?

     c. $2.25 a pound?

28. Coarse gravel sells for $40 a load. Fine gravel sells for $60 a load. How much of each kind of gravel should be used to make

    a. ten loads of a mixture selling for $52 a load?

    b. fifteen loads of a mixture selling for $44 a load?

29. Regular marbles sell at 100 for $2.00. Large marbles (shooters) sell at 25 for $2.00. To the nearest whole marble, how many of each kind should be used to make a package of 100 marbles selling for

    a. $3?

    b. $4?

    c. $5?

    d. $6?

    e. $7?

    f. $8?

30. A bakery sells one kind of doughnut for $2.00 a dozen and another kind for
     $2.50 a dozen. How many of each kind should be used to make

     a. five dozen of a mixture selling for $2.25 a dozen?

     b. ten dozen of a mixture selling for $2.10 a dozen?

     c. five dozen of a mixture selling for $2.40 a dozen?

31. (24-carat gold is pure.) How much 10-carat gold must be combined with how
     much 18-carat gold to have 90 ounces of

     a. 12-carat gold?

     b. 15-carat gold?

     c. 16-carat gold?

32. To have a mixture of 5% sand, 95% topsoil, how much

     a. sand must be added to twenty yards of topsoil?

     b. topsoil must be added to twenty yards of sand?

33. Ms. Brown has fifteen pounds of a candy mixture that sells for $4.25 a pound. It contains only two kinds of candy. One kind sells for $3.50 a pound, and one kind sells for $5.00 a pound.

   a. How many pounds of each kind of candy does it contain?

b–d. Suppose she wants to change the mixture so that it sells for $4.50 a pound.

   b. Which kind of candy should she add?

   c. How much candy should she add?

   d. How many pounds of candy will she end up with?

e–g. Suppose she wants to change the original mixture so that it sells for $3.75 a pound.

   e. Which kind of candy should she add?

   f. How much candy should she add?

   g. How many pounds of candy will she end up with?

34. How much of a 70% sodium hydroxide solution and an 85% sodium hydroxide solution must be combined to have ten liters of a solution that is

    a.   75% sodium hydroxide?

    b.   80% sodium hydroxide?

35. Two kinds of candy sell for $3.50 and $4.75 a pound. How much of each kind should be used to make a mixture of

    a.   ten pounds selling for $4.00 a pound?

    b.   eight pounds selling for $4.25 a pound?

    c.   twelve pounds selling for $3.75 a pound?

36. For each answer to problem 35 that contains a fractional part of a pound, convert your answer to pounds and ounces.

37. A florist sells fifteen dozen roses at a profit of $2.25 a dozen. How many dozen must she sell at a profit of $3.00 a dozen in order to make her average profit $2.55 a dozen?

38. A bird watcher built a bird feeder in his back yard. He has ten pounds of sunflower seeds.

   a–c. How many pounds of other seeds must he add to have a mixture that is

      a. 60% sunflower seeds?

      b. 80% sunflower seeds?

      c. 75% other seeds?

   d–e. Suppose he wants to add sunflower seeds to twenty pounds of a mixture that already contains some sunflower seeds.

      d. If he adds the whole ten pounds and ends up with a mixture that is 80% sunflower seeds, what percent of the twenty-pound mixture was sunflower seeds?

      e. If the twenty-pound mixture is 60% sunflower seeds, how many pounds of sunflower seeds must be added to make the mixture 75% sunflower seeds?

39. A quart of unhomogenized milk is 4% cream, 96% skim milk.

   a–b. Suppose enough cream is added to make the mixture 5% cream, 95% skim milk.

      a. How much cream is added?

      b. What is the total quantity after the addition?

   c–d. Suppose enough skim milk is taken out to make the mixture 5% cream, 95% skim milk.

      c. How much skim milk is taken out?

      d. What is the quantity left after the reduction?

   e–f. Suppose enough skim milk is added to make the mixture 3% cream, 97% skim milk.

      e. How much skim milk is added?

      f. What is the quantity after the addition?

   g–h. Suppose enough cream is taken out to make the mixture 3% cream, 97% skim milk.

      g. How much cream is taken out?

      h. What is the quantity after the reduction?

40. Refer to problem 39 again. How do your answers change if the original quantity is not a quart but is

    a. a liter?

    b. a gallon?

    c. a half-gallon?

41. (Note: The percents given and asked for in this problem refer to weight rather than to number of seeds.) A nursery owner has twenty-five pounds of a grass seed mixture.

    a. She adds ten pounds of Zoysia seed, which makes the mixture 35% Zoysia. What percent of the twenty-five pound mixture was Zoysia?

    b. Suppose the twenty-five pound mixture already contains 10% Zoysia. How much Zoysia must be added to make the mixture contain 40% Zoysia?

    c. Suppose the twenty-five pound mixture contains no Zoysia. How many pounds of a mixture containing 80% Zoysia must be added to make the resulting mixture 60% Zoysia?

42. A beginning chemistry student is ordered to straighten up the chem lab as a
     penalty for making an undue mess of his working area. Three one-liter bottles
     containing alcohol solutions are sitting on a shelf. Bottle A, a 30% solution, is
     one-third full. Bottle B, a 70% solution, is one-fourth full. Bottle C, a 60%
     solution, is one-sixth full. The student decides he might as well do a good job of
     getting the lab in order, and when he sees the three bottles, he

     a. adds enough water to each to fill the bottle. What concentration of
         alcohol is now in each bottle?

     b. combines all the solutions into bottle A and cleans up the other two
         bottles for other uses. What concentration of alcohol is now in bottle A?

  c–d. combines all the solutions into bottle A and then fills bottle A the rest of
         the way with water.

     c. What concentration of alcohol is now in bottle A?

     d. Then he decides it's more convenient for the class to have three
         bottles of solution, so he divides the contents of bottle A equally
         among the three bottles and fills them the rest of the way with
         water. What concentration of alcohol is now in each bottle?

43. A health bar owner sells an 8-ounce glass of orange juice for $1.50, and an 8-ounce glass of grapefruit juice for $2.50. She wants to mix orange juice and grapefruit juice together to make a gallon (128 ounces) of the mixture. How much of each kind of juice should be included if an 8-ounce glass of the mixture is to sell for

     a. $1.75?

     b. $2.00?

     c. $2.25?

44. A delicatessen sells a mixture of two lunch meats for $3.00 a pound. If one kind sells for $2.00 a pound, then about how much does the other kind sell for if, in each pound of the mixture, the first kind weighs

     a.   one-half pound?

     b.   five ounces?

     c.   ten ounces?

45. A butcher wants to grind up enough meat and suet to make one hundred pounds of hamburger. Round steak sells for $2.00 a pound. Chuck steak sells for $1.50 a pound. Suet sells for 25¢ a pound. For this problem, assume (we should be so lucky!) that the round steak and chuck steak contain no suet.

a–c.　How much of each should be used if the suet is to be

　　　a.　20% of the weight and if the hamburger is to sell for $1.50 a pound?

　　　b.　25% of the weight and if the hamburger is to sell for $1.20 a pound?

　　　c.　left out and if the hamburger is to sell for $1.80 a pound?

d–f.　Suppose the suet is to be 25% of the weight. How much should the hamburger sell for if

　　　d.　only the round steak is used?

　　　e.　only the chuck steak is used?

　　　f.　round steak and chuck steak are used in equal amounts?

46. Assume the same facts as in problem 45, except that for each three pounds of meat, the chuck steak already contains five ounces of suet and the round steak already contains three ounces of suet. Also assume that it is possible for the butcher to trim all suet from both kinds of steak if the butcher should wish to do so. Then what are the answers to items a–f?

47.   A tulip grower has determined that an average of 96% of the bulbs she plants
      will germinate, and of those that germinate, 98% will result in a single flower and
      2% will result in two flowers. How many bulbs should she plant in order to have
      15,300 flowers?

48.   20% of the selling price of item A is profit, and 25% of the selling price of item
      B is profit. How much of each kind of item must be sold in order to have an
      average profit of 22% on sales of $100?

49.   A grocer adds 20% to the cost of item A and 25% to the cost of item B in order
      to arrive at the selling prices. To the nearest cent, how much were the sales of
      each kind of item if an average of 22% added to the cost gave total sales of
      $100? (Hint: Your original answers will NOT be whole numbers!)

50. A nursery sells zinnia seeds for $6.00 an ounce and marigold seeds for $8.00 an ounce. How much of each should be used to make a mixture of

    a. one pound selling for $6.50 an ounce?

    b. two pounds selling for $7.50 an ounce?

    c. five pounds selling for $7.25 an ounce?

    d. p pounds selling for $\$s$ an ounce?

51. A nursery sells zinnia seeds for $\$Z$ an ounce and marigold seeds for $\$M$ an ounce.

    a. How much of each kind should be used to make a mixture of p pounds selling for $\$s$ an ounce?

  b-c. There is one condition under which your answer to part a is invalid.

    b. What is this condition?

    c. Assume the condition exists. Then what else must be true? (Hint: Use the condition in your part a original equations.)

52. A nursery sells zinnia seeds for $6.00 an ounce and marigold seeds for $8.00 an ounce. Suppose the zinnia seeds have a 90% germination rate and the marigold seeds have a 95% germination rate. (Hint: To simplify your work, use your answers from problem 50.)

    a–c. What percent of the seeds can be expected to germinate in a mixture of

        a. one pound selling for $6.50 an ounce?

        b. two pounds selling for $7.50 an ounce?

        c. five pounds selling for $7.25 an ounce?

    d–e. Suppose the nursery guarantees that when someone buys flower seeds, the seeds paid for will all germinate. Then how much should the actual weight be when someone pays for

        d. a pound of zinnia seeds?

        e. a pound of marigold seeds?

f-k. Suppose the guarantee of d-e on page 106 is still in effect. Then how much of each kind of seed should be used to make a mixture having

f.   a supposed weight of one pound and selling for $6.50 an ounce?

g.   a supposed weight of two pounds and selling for $7.50 an ounce?

h.   a supposed weight of five pounds and selling for $7.25 an ounce?

i.   an actual weight of one pound and selling for $6.50 an ounce?

j.   an actual weight of two pounds and selling for $7.50 an ounce?

k.   an actual weight of five pounds and selling for $7.25 an ounce?

53. (Give your answers to the nearest whole ounce.) A health bar mixes together several juices to be sold as a health drink. Of the mixture, 10% is carrot juice and 25% is tomato juice. The owner prepares a gallon (128 ounces) of the mixture but then realizes that he has

   a–b.   forgotten to include the carrot juice.

   a.   How much carrot juice should be added to make the carrot juice 10% of the total?

   b.   How much of the complete mixture will there be?

   c–d.   forgotten to include the tomato juice.

   c.   How much tomato juice should be added to make the tomato juice 25% of the total?

   d.   How much of the complete mixture will there be?

   e–f.   included only the tomato juice and the carrot juice.

   e.   How much of the other juices should be added?

   f.   How much of the complete mixture will there be?

54. Refer to problem 53 again.

    a–c. used tomato juice for 25% of the mixture he made but has forgotten to include the carrot juice. In order to have the desired percentages, how much

        a. tomato juice must be added?

        b. carrot juice must be added?

        c. of the total mixture will there be?

    d–f. used carrot juice for 10% of the mixture he made but has forgotten to include the tomato juice. In order to have the desired percentages, how much

        d. carrot juice must be added?

        e. tomato juice must be added?

        f. of the total mixture will there be?

FORMULAS

1. Write a formula to express each rule.

   a. The area A of a rectangle is equal to the product of the rectangle's length l and width w.

   b. The perimeter P of a rectangle is the sum of twice the rectangle's length l and twice the rectangle's width w.

   c. The perimeter P of a rectangle is twice the sum of the rectangle's length l and width w.

   d. The circumference C of a circle is the product of pi and the circle's diameter d.

   e. The area A of a circle is the product of pi and the square of the circle's radius r.

   f. The area A of a triangle is half the product of the triangle's base b and altitude a to that base.

   g. When d dollars are invested at rate r of interest compounded periodically, the amount A accumulated at the end of n periods is the product of the investment and the nth power of the sum of 1 and the interest rate.

2. You are given the formula $A = bc$.

   a–b. Rewrite the given equation to show the effect of each statement. If b is increased by 6 and c is

      a. decreased by 2, then A increases by 15.

      b. increased by 2, then A doubles.

   c–g. What is the effect on A if

      c. b is doubled and c is unchanged?

      d. b is doubled and c is halved?

      e. b is tripled and c is doubled?

      f. b is tripled and c is two-thirds as much (as c was)?

      g. b is three-fourths as much and c is tripled?

   h–i. What is the effect on b if

      h. A is doubled and c is unchanged?

      i. A is two-thirds as much and c is tripled?

3. You are given the formula for the area of a rectangle, $A = lw$, where l and w are in feet.

    a–e. Rewrite the given equation to show the effect of each statement.

    a. If the length increases by 5 feet and the width is unchanged, then the area increases by 40 square feet.

    b. The width is two-thirds of the length.

    c. If five feet is added to the length and if the width is increased by two feet, then the area is doubled.

    d. If the width is increased by six inches and if the length is unchanged, then the area increases by ten square feet.

    e. The area is tripled if eight inches is added to the length and three inches is added to the width.

    f–j. What change takes place in the area if the length is

    f. doubled and the width is halved?

    g. doubled and the width is tripled?

h.   one-fourth as much and the width is two-thirds as much?

i.   one-fourth as much and the width is tripled?

j.   tripled and the width is one-fourth as much?

k–p.   What change takes place in the width if the area is

   k.   doubled and the length is unchanged?

   l.   doubled and the length is doubled?

   m.   doubled and the length is tripled?

   n.   three-fourths as much and the length is doubled?

   o.   doubled and the length is three-fourths as much?

   p.   two-thirds as much and the length is three-fourths as much?

4.   Write a formula for the circumference *C* of a circle in terms of the circle's radius *r*.

5. You are given the formula $A = kr^2$.

    a. How does A change if r is doubled?

    b. How does A change if r is one-third as much?

  c-d. Write an equation to show the effect of each statement.

      c. If r is increased by 2, then A is increased by 30.

      d. If r is decreased by 3, then A is halved.

6. You are given the formula $S = \dfrac{n(n+1)}{2}$. Rewrite the formula to show the effect of each statement.

    a. If n is increased by 1, then S is increased by 15.

    b. If n is increased by 1, then S is increased by $n + 1$.

    c. If n is halved, then S is decreased by 345.

    d. If n is doubled, then S is increased by 26.

7. You are given the formula $D = rt$, where D is the distance traveled, r is the rate of speed, and t is the length of time the rate of speed was maintained. The variables r and t must be consistent. That is, if r is in feet (or meters or yards) per second, then t must be in seconds. Similarly, if r is in units per hour, then t must be in hours. For the following problems, assume that r is in kilometers per hour.

a–e. Rewrite the given equation to show the effect of each statement.

a. If the rate is 10 kph more and the time is an hour less, then the distance is the same.

b. The distance is unchanged if the rate is 15 kph less and the time is two hours more.

c. If the rate is 8 kph more and the time is 30 minutes less, then the distance is 40 kilometers more.

d. If the rate is doubled and if 20 minutes is added to the time, then the distance is 50 kilometers more than twice as much.

e. If ten is added to the rate and subtracted from the time, then the distance decreases by 250 kilometers.

f-k.   What happens to the distance if the rate

    f.   and the time are both doubled?

    g.   is doubled and the time is halved?

    h.   is halved and the time is doubled?

    i.   is two-thirds as much and the time is three-fourths as much?

    j.   is one and a third times as much and the time is one-fourth as much?

    k.   is one and a half times as much and the time is one-fourth as much?

l-o.   What happens to the time if the distance is

    l.   unchanged and the rate is halved?

    m.   doubled and the rate is halved?

    n.   halved and the rate is two-thirds as much?

    o. $\frac{3}{4}$ as much and the rate is $\frac{2}{3}$ as much?

RECTANGLES

8. A rectangle whose perimeter is fifty feet is five feet longer than it is wide.

   a. What are its dimensions?

   b. What is its area?

9. A rectangle's length is three times its width, and its perimeter is forty units.

   a. What are its dimensions?

   b. What is its area?

10. What are the dimensions of a rectangular field if its perimeter is 600 yards and if its width is 50 yards less than its length?

11. 75% of the length of a rectangle and 20% of its width are eliminated. How does the area of the resulting rectangle compare with the area of the original rectangle?

12. The width of a rectangle is 30% less than its length. Its perimeter is 68 cm.

    a. What are its dimensions?

    b. What is its area?

13. The length of a rectangle is 40% more than its width. Its area is 560 square centimeters.

    a. What are its dimensions?

    b. What is its perimeter?

14. The perimeter of a rectangle is three times its length. Its area is 800 square units. What are its dimensions?

15. The width of a rectangle is 40 cm less than its perimeter. The rectangle's area is 102 square cm.

    a. What are the rectangle's dimensions?

    b. What is the rectangle's perimeter?

16. A rectangle is twice as long as it is wide. If its area is 288 square units, what are its dimensions?

17. A rectangle is three centimeters longer than it is wide. If its length were to be decreased by two centimeters, its area would decrease by thirty square centimeters.

    a. What are its dimensions?

    b. What is its area?

18. A rectangular flower bed is five feet longer than it is wide. Its area is eighty-four square feet.

    a. What are its dimensions?

    b-d. The flower bed has an eighteen-inch verbena border (immediately inside).

        b. What is the area (in square feet) of the border?

        c. What is the area of the rest of the flower bed?

        d. What are the dimensions of the rest of the flower bed?

19. A nursery owner has a rectangular area 50 feet by 60 feet planted in shrubs. Because of a large demand for his shrubs, he decides to triple the area by planting shrubs in strips of equal width along two adjacent sides of the rectangle.

   a. How wide must the strip be?

   b. What are the dimensions of the new rectangle?

   c. What is the area of the new rectangle?

20. A rectangle having an area of 120 square inches is drawn on a sheet of paper. Inside this rectangle, another rectangle having an area of 48 square inches is drawn, leaving a space two inches wide all around between it and the larger rectangle. What are the dimensions of

   a. the larger rectangle?

   b. the smaller rectangle?

21. The area of a rectangle is 126 square centimeters and its perimeter is 46 centimeters. What are its dimensions?

22. A rectangle whose length is three times its width has a perimeter of 80 cm. A strip 3 cm wide is then cut off two adjacent sides of the rectangle.

   a. What is the area of the part that was cut off the rectangle?

   b. What are the dimensions of the new rectangle?

23. Dave and Miguel agree to share equally the work of painting a wall that is fifteen feet long and eight feet high. If Dave paints a border of uniform width around the edges of the wall and Mike paints the rest, how wide should the border be?

24. A rectangular field is sixty feet longer than it is wide. One side borders a neighbor's property that is already fenced. How many yards of fencing are needed to fence the other three sides if the area of the field is 72,000 square feet?

25. The length of a rectangle is two meters more than its width. If its area is 255 square meters, what are its dimensions?

26. An engineer whose hobby is gardening set aside a rectangular plot in her (large!) back yard for a flower garden. The rectangle was twice as long as it was wide and had an area of 2,450 square feet. Then she decided that her friends wouldn't be able to see the flowers properly unless they could get closer than the outer edges of the rectangle, so she had a three-foot-wide sidewalk constructed all around the (inside) edge of the rectangle, and she also had a three-foot-wide sidewalk running down the center from one long edge to the other.

    a.   What were the dimensions of the whole rectangle?

b–d.   There were two smaller rectangles left (after the sidewalks) for the flower garden.

    b.   What were the dimensions of each of these smaller rectangles?

    c.   What was the area of each of these smaller rectangles?

    d.   What was the total area of the sidewalk(s)?

27. A rectangle having a width four inches less than its length is drawn inside
   another rectangle and shaded in. The length of the larger rectangle is twice its
   width. What are the dimensions of each rectangle if the unshaded area in the
   larger rectangle is

   a. 68 square inches and the area of the smaller rectangle is 60 square
       inches?

   b. 221 square inches and the width of the larger rectangle equals the length
       of the smaller rectangle?

   c. 29 square inches and the perimeter of the larger rectangle is 10 inches
       more than the perimeter of the smaller rectangle?

   d. 210 square inches and the width of the larger rectangle is three inches
       more than the length of the smaller rectangle?

   e. 20 square inches and the unshaded area forms a frame one inch wide on
       each of the four sides around the shaded area?

    f.   53 square inches and the perimeter of the smaller rectangle is 28 inches?

    g.   116 square inches and the length of the larger rectangle equals the perimeter of the smaller rectangle?

    h.   equal to the shaded area and the width of the smaller rectangle is three-fourths the width of the larger rectangle?

    i.   twice as much as the shaded area and the perimeter of the smaller rectangle is 32 inches less than the perimeter of the larger rectangle?

    j.   six times as much in square inches as the perimeter of the larger rectangle is in inches, and the length of the smaller rectangle is equal to the width of the larger rectangle?

    k.   seven times as much in square inches as the perimeter of the smaller rectangle is in inches, and the width of the larger rectangle is two inches more than the length of the smaller rectangle?

28. One rectangle is two inches longer and one inch wider than another. The sum of their areas is 286 square inches, and the difference between their areas is 34 square inches.

    a-b.   What are the dimensions of

        a.   the larger rectangle?

        b.   the smaller rectangle?

    c-d.   What is the area of

        c.   the larger rectangle?

        d.   the smaller rectangle?

29. A rectangle has an area of 576 square inches. Find its dimensions if

    a.   its area is the same when the width is three inches less and the length is sixteen inches more.

    b.   its area is 27 square inches more when its length is increased by three inches.

    c.   its area is 144 square inches less when its width is decreased by two inches.

30. A rectangle has an area of 576 square inches. What are its dimensions if

   a. it is twenty inches longer than it is wide?

   b. its width is fourteen inches less than its length?

   c. its length and width are equal?

31. The area of a rectangle is 360 square units. If one unit is added to both the length and the width of the rectangle, the new area is 400 square units. What are the dimensions of the (original) rectangle?

32. The length of a rectangle is four times its width. A disk having a radius of six inches is placed inside the rectangle, leaving the rectangle with an uncovered area of 756 square inches.

   a. What are the exact dimensions of the rectangle? (Hint: They are strange-looking numbers, so don't panic.)

   b. Using pi = $3\frac{1}{7}$, what are the dimensions of the rectangle? (Hint: The numbers still don't look exactly ordinary, but they aren't as bad as in part a.)

33. A sidewalk of uniform width surrounds a rectangular building.

   a. How wide is the sidewalk if the building is forty feet by fifty feet and the area of the sidewalk is five hundred seventy-six square feet?

   b. What is the area of the sidewalk if the building is forty feet by fifty feet and the sidewalk is four feet wide?

   c. How wide is the sidewalk if the building is ten feet longer than wide, if the outside perimeter of the sidewalk is one hundred ninety-two feet, and if the area of the sidewalk is seven hundred four square feet?

   d. What is the perimeter of the building if the sidewalk is four feet wide and has an area of six hundred forty-eight square feet?

   e. What are the dimensions of the building if its width is two-thirds its length, and if the sidewalk is five feet wide and covers an area of eight hundred square feet?

D = rt

Keep the formula $D = rt$ in mind for all problems. Don't hesitate to manipulate it if it makes solving the problem easier: $r = \frac{D}{t}$ or $t = \frac{D}{r}$. If an answer is not a whole number, then write the fractional part as a fraction rather than as a decimal or a decimal approximation.

34. Porter drove for three hours at 40 kph and for two hours at 50 kph. What was her average speed during that time?

35. A car traveled from A to B at 50 kph, from B to C at 60 kph, and returned (C to B to A) at 80 kph. What was the average speed (1) on the outbound trip and (2) on the round trip if the distances from A to B and from B to C were, respectively,

    a.   100 km and 120 km?

    b.   300 km and 300 km?

    c.   120 km and 100 km?

36. During the first half of a trip, Kum averaged 60 kph. His average for the entire trip was 66 kph. What was his average for the last half of the trip?

37. A driver completed a trip in six hours. If his average speed had been ten kph more, the trip would have taken one hour less.

     a. What was the average speed for the trip?

     b. How far did the driver go?

38. It took three hours and forty minutes for a car traveling at 60 kph to go from A to B.

     a. How long will the return trip take if the car travels at 80 kph?

     b. What must be the car's average speed from B to A if the return trip is to be made in two and a half hours?

39. A road runs parallel to a railroad track. A car traveling an average speed of 50 kph starts out on the road at noon. One hour later, a train traveling an average speed of 90 kph in the same direction (as the car) passes the spot where the car started. If the car and the train continue to travel along parallel paths, what time will the train overtake the car?

40. A tornado usually travels at 25 to 40 miles an hour. If you see a tornado
     approaching from half a mile away, how much time does that give you to take
     cover?

41. Two jetliners would fly at the same speed in still air. They leave an airport at
     the same time and fly in the same air current but in opposite directions. The
     jetliner going with the air current is 1,470 miles from the airport three hours
     after takeoff. The jetliner going against the air current is 2,050 miles from the
     airport five hours after takeoff. What is the speed of the

     a. air current?

     b. jetliners in still air?

42. It took Dana six minutes to circle a quarter-mile track three times. What was
     her average speed in mph?

43. A car traveled a distance of 100 miles. If its average speed had been 8 mph
     more, the trip would have taken 25 minutes less. What was the car's average
     speed?

44. Two canoeists paddle at the same rate in still water. One canoeist paddled upstream for an hour and a half and was eighteen miles from the starting point. The other canoeist paddled downstream for two hours and was thirty-six miles from the starting point.

    a. What was the speed of the current?

    b. At what speed do the canoeists paddle in still water?

45. A driver averaged a speed of 20 kph more on a trip from A to B than on the return trip. The return trip took one and a half times as long. What was the average speed of the trip from

    a. A to B?

    b. B to A?

46. A runner averaged 8 kph during a race. If she had averaged 1 kph more, she would have finished in 20 minutes less.

    a. How long did it take the runner to finish the race?

    b. How many kilometers long was the race?

47. A driver drove at 80 kph for 20 minutes of a one-hour trip. His average speed for the whole trip was 75 kph. What was his average speed for the other 40 minutes of the trip?

48. A car passes point A going 60 kph. Fifteen minutes later a second car going in the same direction passes point A going 80 kph. Assuming that both cars are maintaining a constant speed and continue on the same highway,

   a. how long will it be before the second car catches up to the first car?

   b. how far from point A will the two cars be when the second car catches up to the first car?

49. Amy and George are long-distance runners. Amy started out at noon to run a thirty-mile course. George started out half an hour later. If Amy's average speed is eight miles an hour and George's is ten miles an hour,

   a. how many minutes ahead of Amy will George finish the race?

   b. at what time will George pass Amy?

50. A driver traveled from A to B. On the return trip, he averaged 10 kph more and that trip took 30 minutes less. If he had averaged 10 kph less on the outgoing trip, that trip would have taken 40 minutes more.

   a–b. On the trip from A to B,

      a. what was the average speed?

      b. how much time did it take?

   c–d. On the trip from B to A,

      c. what was the average speed?

      d. how much time did it take?

51. A jetliner flew against a head wind from Detroit to Los Angeles, a distance of about 2,000 miles, in $4\frac{1}{2}$ hours. The return trip at the same engine speed and same wind velocity (tail wind this time) took 4 hours.

   a. What was the wind velocity?

   b. What would be the jetliner's speed in still air?

52. A skier averaged 30 kph for two minutes on one slope and 40 kph for ninety seconds on another slope.

    a. How far did he travel?

    b. What was his average speed for the two slopes combined?

53. An automobile traveled 360 km. If its average speed had been 2 kph more, the trip would have taken 18 minutes less.

    a. What was its average speed?

    b. How long did the trip take?

54. A driver averaged 80 kph on the first of five laps on a test track. What must be his average speed on the other four laps in order to have an overall average of 100 kph for the five laps?

55. Ms. Carter drove from A to B at 60 kph. She drove at 80 kph on the return trip. What was her average speed for the round trip?

56. A skier averaged 40 kph on the first half of a slope and 30 kph the rest of the way. What was her overall average speed?

57. A skier averaged 40 kph on the first third of a slope and 30 kph the rest of the way. What was his overall average speed?

58. A skier averaged 40 kph on the first third of a slope, 30 kph on the next third, and 20 kph the rest of the way. What was her overall average speed?

59. Ms. Wuli drove from A to B. If her average speed had been 8 kph more, the trip would have taken an hour less. If her average speed had been $3\frac{1}{2}$ kph less, the trip would have taken half an hour more.

    a. How much time did the trip take?

    b. What was her average speed?

    c. What is the distance from A to B?

60. In order to qualify for a race, a car must complete two laps of a five-mile track at an average speed of 120 mph. Davi's car averaged only 90 mph during the first lap.

    a. How fast must the car go during the second lap in order to qualify for the race?

    b. What is your answer to a above if the average speed on the first lap was 60 mph instead of 90 mph?

61. Car A started out from City A and headed toward City B. One hour later, Car B started out from City B and headed toward City A. The two cars passed each other 35 miles from City B. Both cars started out at the same time on their return trips, and they passed each other 60 miles from City A.

    a–b. If the two cars traveled at the same rate of speed,

        a. how far is City A from City B?

        b. what was their rate of speed?

    c–d. If car A traveled only five-sixths as fast as car B,

        c. how far apart are the two cities?

        d. what was each car's rate of speed?

62. Alma and Belinda are to run a race over a five-mile course. Alma runs faster than Belinda, however, so in order to be fair they have agreed that Belinda will have a head start.

   a–b. In minutes and seconds, how much of a head start should Belinda be given if her usual speed is

   a. 8 mph and Alma's is 10 mph?

   b. two-thirds of Alma's? (Hint: The answer is in terms of Alma's speed.)

   c–d. Suppose Belinda is given a five-minute head start. Who will win the race, and by how much time, if

   c. Belinda's speed is 6 mph and Alma's is 9 mph?

   d. Belinda's speed is three-fourths of Alma's speed?

63. Two equally matched canoeists were to race up a river and back. There was quiet water along one bank, but a slight current ran through the rest of the river. A took the bank, B the center, figuring that the time B lost going upstream would be regained going downstream. Were they right? That is, did they finish in a tie? If not, who won? Or isn't there enough information given to determine the answers?

REMINDERS (PERCENTS & WORK RATES)

The interest rate an investment earns is understood to be an annual rate unless otherwise specified. *Simple interest* is interest that is not compounded. If you invest $1000 at 6% simple interest, your interest is $60 a year whether you receive it each year or whether you let it accumulate along with the $1000 principal.

$A = P(1 + r)^n$ is the amount you will have at the end of n periods at a compound interest rate of r% per period if you invest P dollars at the beginning and leave it there.

Example 1: You invest $1,000 at 8% compounded annually. At the end of ten years, you will have $A = 1000(1.08)^{10}$.

Example 2: You invest $1,000 at 8% compounded quarterly. At the end of ten years, you will have $A = 1000(1.02)^{40}$.

If it takes Ann A hours to do a job, then she will do $\frac{1}{A}$ of the job in one hour, and she will do $h(\frac{1}{A}) = \frac{h}{a}$ of the job in h hours. If it takes Bob B hours to do the job, then he and Ann working together on the job will do $\frac{1}{A} + \frac{1}{B}$ of the job in one hour.

Example 3: It takes Ann two hours, and Bob three hours, to do a job if each works alone. How long will it take them if they work together? Answer: Put h = the number of hours the job will take.

$$\text{Then } \frac{1}{2} + \frac{1}{3} = \frac{1}{h} \text{ so } \frac{5}{6} = \frac{1}{h} \text{ and } h = 1\frac{1}{5}.$$

PERCENTS

1. Charles scored 75% on a test and got six problems wrong. How many problems were on the test?

2. A butcher adds 25% to the cost of meat in order to arrive at a selling price. What is the cost of the meat sold if the selling price totals $100?

3. A total of 40% of Ms. Becker's gross pay is withheld for various taxes. If Ms. Becker receives $135, what was her gross pay?

4. A fan was purchased at a discount of 30% for $21. What was the price of the fan before the discount?

5. 85% of all cars sold in Chicago are some color other than black. If three hundred black cars were sold in Chicago, how many cars were sold there?

6. A rubber band stretches to 350% of its original length. What is the original length of the rubber band if it is $10\frac{1}{2}$ inches long when stretched?

7. 60% of a senior class are males. There are 44 females in the class. How many people are in the class?

8. Jorge's pay after 7% was deducted for social security tax and 15% was deducted for federal income tax was $117.

    a. What was Jorge's pay before the deductions?

    b. How much was deducted for social security tax?

    c. How much was deducted for federal income tax?

9. A federal excise tax of 10% is assessed on sales of certain "luxury" items. If a "luxury" item, including the tax, sells for $14,855.50, how much is

    a. the item?

    b. the excise tax?

10. A state income tax is 5% of taxable income.

    a. How much taxable income will it take to require an income tax of $950?

    b-c. Suppose the amount of taxable income, less the income tax due, amounts to $23,750. Then how much is

       b. the taxable income?

       c. the income tax due?

11. The Ashtons always give 10% of their gross income to their church. If their gross income, less the amount of their contribution, was $190.17, how much was their gross income?

12. Over a certain number of days, weather forecaster A forecasted correctly 80% of the time, and weather forecaster B forecasted correctly 70% of the time. If the number of incorrect forecasts of A and B are added, the sum is 30. How many days were involved?

13. A store is selling everything at a 25% discount. What was the original selling price if the store's

    a.   total receipts are $1,500?

    b.   total discounts given are $1,500?

14. An invoice from Kayman Co. said that 2% could be deducted if the invoice was paid within ten days. After deducting the 2% when the invoice was paid five days later, the (correct) amount of the remittance was $100. 42. What was the amount of the invoice?

15. Hamburger selling at $1.25 a pound contains 30% fat. How much does the consumer pay for the meat without the fat?

16. A jeweler bought some necklaces and bracelets for $1,100. The cost of the necklaces was 20% more than the cost of the bracelets. How much did the jeweler pay for

    a.   the necklaces?

    b.   the bracelets?

17. A box of grass seed will seed 500 square feet with a 95% germination rate. How many boxes of seed should be used to seed 1,900 square feet if an effect of a 100% germination rate is desired?

18. A state tax of 4% and a federal tax of 3% was assessed on all telephone calls for the month. The total bill for calls and taxes was $12.57. How much was for

    a. calls alone?

    b. state tax?

    c. federal tax?

19. Simple interest at the rate of 10% is charged on a loan. Suppose $3,000 was paid

    a. for interest on a two-year loan. How much was the loan?

    b-c. to pay in full a two-year loan, including all interest. How much was the

       b. loan?

       c. interest?

20. A real estate agent charged a commission of 8% on the selling price of a house. In addition to this expense, there were other seller's expenses of $350. After all expenses, the seller, who had invested $30,000 in the house, made a profit of $470. What was the

   a. selling price of the house?

   b. real estate agent's commission on the sale?

21. Out of a gross amount earned weekly by Mr. Loring, 7% is deducted for social security tax, 20% for federal income tax, 5% for state income tax, $1\frac{1}{2}$% for city income tax, $5 for union dues, and $25 for a savings plan. Mr. Loring's net pay last week was $236.

   a. What was his gross pay?

   b-e. How much was deducted for

      b. social security tax?

      c. federal income tax?

      d. state income tax?

      e. city income tax?

22. Ms. Andrews invested $3,000 at 6% simple interest and $4,000 at a different rate of simple interest. If her yearly interest income on these investments is $500, what rate of interest does the $4,000 earn?

23. A grocer bought a crate of grapefruit and a crate of eggs for a total of $45. The eggs cost $25 more than the grapefruit. If 30% is to be added to the cost of the grapefruit and 20% to the cost of the eggs in order to arrive at a selling price, then

   a. what was the grocer's cost of the eggs?

   b. what was the grocer's cost of the grapefruit?

   c. what will be the grocer's selling price of the eggs?

   d. what will be the grocer's selling price of the grapefruit?

24. Silver has appreciated in value 10% for each of the past five years. If Ms. Ordon invested $2,000 in silver five years ago, how much is her investment worth now?

25. Suppose you put $5,000 in a savings account that earns interest at 9%. How much will it be worth at the end of a year if the interest is

    a. simple interest?

    b. compounded annually?

    c. compounded semiannually?

    d. compounded quarterly?

    e. compounded monthly?

    f. compounded daily, counting 360 days per year?

26. Mr. Marler invests $10,000 in a time savings account that earns interest at 8%. Interest is paid semiannually. Instead of taking the interest each time it is due, Mr. Marler elects to let it accumulate along with his original investment. How much will be in the account at the end of five years, if the interest accumulated also earns interest?

27. Suppose you put $1,000 in a savings account and let the interest accumulate. At the end of five years, how much will be in the account if 6% interest is paid and is

    a. not compounded?

    b. compounded annually?

    c. compounded semiannually?

    d. compounded quarterly?

    e. compounded monthly?

28. Ms. Lambert invested an amount at 8% interest. At the end of two years, the total (including interest) was $2,320. How much was her initial investment if the interest was

    a. simple interest?

    b. compounded annually?

    c. compounded semiannually?

    d. compounded quarterly?

29. Marla had 30 more problems right than wrong on a test and scored 80% on it. How many problems

    a. were on the test?

    b. did she get right?

    c. did she get wrong?

30. If the numerator of a fraction is decreased by 25% and the denominator is increased by 25%, the resulting fraction is $\frac{3}{10}$. What is the original fraction?

31. Suppose an investment pays a rate of 8% compounded semiannually. How much must be invested now in order to have $10,000 accumulated at the end of ten years?

32. Mr. Chatham's investments earn simple interest, some at 10% and the rest at 8%. The yearly interest totals $930. If the amounts invested had been reversed, the yearly interest would have been $60 less. How much is invested at each rate?

33. Ms. Chou bought 100 shares of stock at $30 a share plus a broker's commission of 2% of the purchase price. When she sold the stock, the broker's commission was 2% of the selling price. If her profit was $370, how much was

    a. her selling price per share?

    b. the broker's commission on the selling price?

34. Mr. Leonardo invested part of $6,000 at 6% and the rest at 9%. How much was invested at each rate if the overall return was 8%?

35. A loan company made two one-year loans to Ms. Martin. One loan was at 10% simple interest, and the other was at 15% simple interest. The total of the two loans was $4,000. The amount of interest Ms. Martin owed at the end of a year was $475. How much was each loan?

36. An income tax chart shows the tax on income between $6,000 and $10,000 to be $1,080 plus 22% of the income over $6,000. Mr. Jason's income tax was $1,465. How much was his income?

37. Mr. Landry invested $10,000 at simple interest. Part earned 6% and the rest earned 7%. The annual income from these investments was $660. How much was each investment?

38. The Cartwrights took out two loans totaling $10,000. The interest on one of the loans was 8%, and the interest on the other was 10%. How much was borrowed at each rate, and how much was the interest on each loan, if

   a. the total interest came to $950 a year?

   b. the overall interest rate was 8.5%?

39. Michigan assesses a 4% sales tax on certain retailed items. A retailer finds she has collected a total of $1,035.87 for

   a. tax. What was the total on which the tax was charged?

   b-c. tax and taxable items. How much of the total was for

   b. taxable items?

   c. tax?

40. Ms. Akers sold $10,000 of A and B merchandise last month. Her commissions are 8% on A merchandise.

   a-b. Her commissions are 12% on B merchandise. How much of each kind did she sell if her total commissions were

      a. $1,080?

      b. $980?

   c-d. What percent are her commissions on B merchandise if

      c. her total commissions were $860 and her sales of B merchandise were $3,000?

      d. her sales of A merchandise were $2,000 and her total commissions were $880?

41. A supermarket made a profit of 25% of the selling price of meat and a profit of 5% of the selling price of detergent. If the cost of the meat and detergent sold yesterday was $300.10 and the selling price was $350,

      a. what was the selling price of each?

      b. what was the cost of each?

42. Two items were on sale, one at 15% off, and one at 20% off. Ms. Porter paid a total of $32.90 for the two items, whose regular price (total) was $40.

   a.   What was the regular price of each item?

   b.   What was the sale price of each item?

43. A fifty-pound crate of apples cost $12. Experience shows that 10% of the apples will spoil. For how much a pound should the apples be sold in order to show a profit of 20% of the selling price?

44. The Dulims took out two loans, one of which was one and a half times as large as the other. The interest rate on the larger loan was three-fourths the interest rate on the smaller loan. The loans totaled $12,000, and the interest totaled $1,020.

   a.   How much was each loan?

   b.   What was the interest rate on each loan?

   c.   How much was the interest on each loan?

45. Mr. Archer paid $33 for two pairs of slacks on sale. The discount was 25% on one pair and was 40% on the other pair. The regular prices totaled $50. How much

    a.   was the regular price of each pair?

    b.   did he pay for each pair?

46. 25% of the tickets to a play were sold at a discount of 20% from the regular price. What was the regular price of a ticket if a total of

    a.   200 tickets were sold for $570?

    b.   460 tickets were sold for $1,092.50?

    c.   t tickets were sold for $d?

47. Midstate assesses a 3% retail sales tax on some items. A shopper paid $100, of which $52 was for nontaxable items. How much was the shopper charged for

    a.   taxable items?

    b.   sales tax?

48. Over a certain ten-year period, the annual inflation rate was 6%. If the cost of an article was $1,000 at the

   a. beginning of that period, how much was its cost at the end of the period?

   b. end of that period, how much was its cost at the beginning of the period?

49. Ms. Bowen's bank pays interest on savings accounts at 6% compounded quarterly. Suppose Ms. Bowen deposited a certain amount and left it there for ten years. How much

   a. was in the account at the end of the ten years if she deposited $1,000?

   b. did she deposit if the account was worth $1,000 at the end of the ten years?

50. From list prices, discounts are given of 40% to A and 35% to B. The (discounted) total sales last week to A and B were $7,000. If the sales to A had been made to B, and vice versa, the total would have been $500 less. What was the list price of the items sold to A? to B?

51. Correct to one decimal place, what annual interest rate has been earned if $1,000 invested five years ago is now worth $1,469.33 and the interest has been compounded

    a.   annually?

    b.   semiannually?

    c.   quarterly?

52. Ms. Reynoso has borrowed $2,000. Interest on the unpaid balance is to be compounded at 10%, and the loan will be paid in full at the end of five years. How much will she have to pay each time, and how much will she have paid at the end of the five years, if

    a.   only one payment is to be made, and that at the end of the five years?

    b.   five approximately equal payments are to be made, one at the end of each year? (See the hint below.)

    c.   sixty approximately equal payments are to be made, one at the end of each month? (See the hint below.)

Hint: You may find the following formula helpful: $x^n + x^{n-1} + x^{n-2} + \ldots + x^2 + x + 1 = \dfrac{x^{n+1} - 1}{x - 1}$

53. (Hint: The knowledge you gained from doing problem 52 is helpful here.)
    Yoshio, a mechanical engineer, has just graduated from college and has been
    offered a good job. He figures that he will earn $40,000 a year within a few
    years and also that $40,000 a year will be a comfortable retirement income, so
    he plans to put a given amount into a retirement fund at the end of each year so
    that he will be able to draw $40,000 a year from it when he retires.

    He turned 22 on January 1 and plans to retire when he is 62 and to start drawing
    from the fund at the end of that year. The life expectancy of a 62-year-old
    male is 17 years. Assume that amounts in the fund will earn compound interest at
    9% annually for as long as the fund exists.

    a. How much (total) should Yoshio expect to be able to withdraw from the
        fund, assuming he has put enough in to realize his goal?

    b. How much will Yoshio need to have in the fund when he retires?

    c. How much should Yoshio put into the fund each year in order to have the
        needed amount in the fund when he is 62?

    d-e. Now suppose that the annual inflation rate is 5%.

    d. $40,000 a year now would be equivalent to how much 40 years from now?

    e. Assuming inflation stops once Yoshio reaches 62 (he should be so
        lucky!), how much will he need to have in the fund when he is 62, and
        how much should he put into the fund each year? (Answer parts b
        and c again for the new figure from d.)

WORK RATES

54. Assume that all masons work at the same rate of speed. If it takes eight masons (all working at the same time) fifteen days to do a job, how long will it take for the job to be done by

    a.   ten masons?

    b.   four masons?

    c.   three masons?

    d.   sixteen masons?

55. Suppose that the amount of water that can flow through two pipes is directly proportional to the squares of their radii. Pipe A has a radius of three inches. Water flows through it at the rate of 150 gallons a second.

At what rate will water flow through pipe B if pipe B

    a.   has a radius of four inches?

    b.   has a radius of two inches?

    c.   has a diameter of ten inches?

    d.   has a diameter of nine inches?

56. Harold and Jem together can do a job in six days. Harold can do the job working alone in eight days. How long does it take Jem to do the job working alone?

57. It takes four minutes to fill a bath tub if the hot and cold water taps are both on and the stopper is in. It takes six minutes to empty the tub if the taps are off and the stopper is out. How long does it take to fill the tub if both taps are on and the stopper is out?

58. Two bricklayers working together can do a job in eight days. One of the bricklayers takes twelve days to do the job alone. How long does it take the other bricklayer to do the job?

59. Laura works twice as fast as Marta. If it takes them ten hours to do a job working together, how long does it take each person to do the job working alone?

60. A 15,000-gallon water tank can be filled in twenty minutes by means of two intake pipes, one of which allows a 40% greater flow than the other. At what rate does the water flow through each of the two pipes?

61. Freda and Ann together can do a job in nine days. Freda works two-thirds as fast as Ann. How long does it take each one to do the job working alone?

62. Jeff takes 40% longer than Ken to do a job. Jeff and Ken working together can do the job in thirty-five hours. How long does it take each of them working alone to do the job?

63. If Jai can do a job in twelve days and Peter can do the job in twenty-four days, how long will it take to finish

    a. the whole job if they work together on it?

    b–d. the last part of the job if

        b. Jai works alone for three days, and then Peter joins him?

        c. Peter works alone for three days, and then Jai joins him?

        d. Jai works alone for two days, and then Peter works with him for three days, and then Peter works alone?

64. It took Karl and Louis eight hours to do a job together. If Karl had worked only half as fast and Louis had worked twice as fast, they would have needed ten hours to do the job. How long does it take each one to do the job alone?

65. Working together, Carole and Katherine can complete a job in twenty hours. Carole works 25% faster than Katherine. How long does it take each of them to do the job working alone?

66. Jim and Frank together can do a job in six days. Jim and Tony together can do the job in seven and a half days. Tony and Frank together can do the job in ten days. How long does it take to do the job if

    a.   each person works alone?

    b.   all three people work together?

67. The stopper is in the (large!) bath tub. It takes nine minutes to fill the tub if only the hot water tap is turned on, and it takes six minutes to fill the tub if only the cold water tap is turned on. Once the tub is filled and the taps are turned off, it takes ten minutes to empty the tub. How long does it take to fill the tub if

    a.   the stopper is out and only the cold water tap is turned on?

    b.   the stopper is out and only the hot water tap is turned on?

    c.   the stopper is in and both taps are turned on?

    d.   the stopper is out and both taps are turned on?

68. Marty can do a job in ten hours. After working for an hour, he is joined by Nat, who works two-thirds as fast as Marty. How long does it take them to finish the job?

69. Letitia and Jennifer working together can complete a job in ten hours. Letitia starts working alone and has half of the job done by the time Jennifer joins her eight hours later. How long does it take

    a.   Letitia to do the job alone?

    b.   the two girls to finish the job?

    c.   Jennifer to do the job alone?

70. Working together, a job takes Tom and Joe 8 days, Tom and Dave $13\frac{1}{3}$ days, and Joe and Dave $6\frac{2}{3}$ days. How long does it take each person to do the job alone?

71. Betty works three-fourths as fast as Kitty, who can do a job in 9 hours. If Kitty works for 4 hours before Betty joins her, how much longer does it take them to finish the job?

72.   A large water tank has two intake pipes and one drainpipe.

a–d.   The larger intake pipe can fill the tank in 20 minutes. The smaller intake pipe can fill the tank in 30 minutes. The drainpipe can empty the tank in 40 minutes. How long does it take to fill the tank if

a.   the valves of both intake pipes are open and the drainpipe valve is closed?

b.   the valves of the larger intake pipe and the drainpipe are open and the other valve is closed?

c.   the valves of the smaller intake pipe and the drainpipe are open and the other valve is closed?

d.   all three valves are open?

e–h.   The larger intake pipe can fill the tank in 20 minutes. The two intake pipes working together can fill the tank in 15 minutes. If the valve of the larger intake pipe is closed but the valves of the smaller intake pipe and the drainpipe are open, the tank can be filled in 4 hours. How long does it take

e.   the smaller pipe working alone to fill the tank?

(continued on next page)

    f.   to drain the tank when the two intake valves are closed?

    g.   to fill the tank if the valve of the smaller pipe is closed but the other two valves are open?

    h.   to fill the tank if all three valves are open?

73. If Lyle and Theresa work together, the work gets done in 25% less time than would be expected. (For example, if it takes one person 20 hours to do the work and it takes the other person 30 hours, then in one hour they would do $\frac{1}{20} + \frac{1}{30}$ $= \frac{1}{12}$ of the job, so the job would be expected to take 12 hours if they work together. 25% of 12 = 3, so the work would be done in 12 – 3 = 9 hours if they work together.)

    a.   They worked together for six hours, completing two-thirds of the job, and then Lyle worked another six hours to finish the job. How long does it take each person working alone to do the job?

    b.   Lyle can do the job in sixteen hours. It takes six hours to do the job when he works with Theresa. How long does it take Theresa to do the job alone?

    c.   If they work together, the job can be done in fifteen hours. How long does it take Lyle to do the job alone if it takes Theresa thirty hours to do the job alone?

d–e.   Lyle can do the job in fifteen hours. He works for five hours. Then Theresa helps and the job is completed in another three hours. How long does the job take if

    d.   they work together on it all the way through?

    e.   Theresa works alone?

    f.   Lyle worked for two hours. Then Theresa helped for three hours, at which point the job was three-fifths done. Theresa finished up alone in another four hours. How long does it take each one to do the job alone?

g–h.   Theresa worked for three hours. Then Lyle helped for two hours, at which point the job was two-fifths done. If the job was nine-tenths done after they worked together for another four hours, how long would it take

    g.   to do the job if they worked together on it all the way through?

    h.   each of them do the job alone?

MISCELLANEOUS

1. Five more than twice a number is 87. What is the number?

2. The sum of two consecutive integers is 79. What are the integers?

3. The sum of two consecutive even numbers is 150. What are the numbers?

4. What two consecutive odd numbers have a sum of 64?

5. The perimeter of an equilateral triangle is 48. How long is a side?

6. The length of a rectangle is 25 cm. Its perimeter is 80 cm. How wide is it?

7. If half of a given number is added to three times the given number, the result is 63. What is the number?

8. A giant pizza was to be shared among three people in the ratio of 2:3:5. If the pizza was cut into thirty pieces, how many pieces did each person get?

9. Al had one-fourth of the problems on a test wrong. He had thirty-six problems right. How many problems were on the test?

10. An isosceles triangle has a base of 8 cm and a perimeter of 44 cm. What are the lengths of its legs?

11. A truck has been hired to cart away a large pile of rocks weighing twenty (short) tons. How many trips must the truck make if it can carry 2,500 pounds of rocks in one trip?

12. A car travels 300 km in five hours and goes another 300 km at 50 kph. What is

    a. the time taken for the 600 km?

    b. the average speed of the car for the 600 km?

13. 40% of a junior class are girls. There are 84 boys in the class. How many members does the class have?

14. The sum of three consecutive integers is 78. What are the integers?

15. A farmer uses 304 acres of land for soybeans, corn, and wheat in the ratio of 4:1:3. How many acres are used for each crop?

16. The sum of two consecutive even numbers is 66. What are the numbers?

17. A typist charged 75¢ a page for typing a manuscript. Her total charge was $86.25. How many pages were in the manuscript?

18. A positive number is sixteen times as great as its reciprocal. What is the number?

19. A square having an area of nine square cm is centered inside a square having an area of twenty-five square cm. How much space is between the larger square and the smaller square on each side? (Hint: Draw a picture. How long is a side of the larger square? How long is a side of the smaller square?)

20. A city income tax of 2% is assessed on taxable income. If the Cartwrights' assessed city income tax is $375, what is their taxable income?

21. After 21% had been deducted for taxes, Formica's pay was $82.95. How much was

    a. Formica's pay before taxes were deducted?

    b. deducted for taxes?

22. Three times a number plus half as much again is 72. What is the number?

23. What is the radius of a circle whose area is 225π square cm?

24. The formula for converting Celsius degrees to Fahrenheit degrees is $F = \frac{9}{5}C + 32$.

    a. The standard Fahrenheit boiling point for water is 212°. What is the standard Celsius boiling point for water?

    b. The standard Fahrenheit freezing point for water is 32°. What is the standard Celsius freezing point for water?

    c. The normal Fahrenheit temperature for a human body is 98.6°. How much is this on the Celsius scale?

    d. On a summer day when the Fahrenheit temperature is 80° or more, what is the Celsius temperature?

25. A plumber worked ten hours at $15 an hour. How many hours does she have to work at $20 an hour in order to average $18 an hour?

26. A waitress has averaged 60¢ in tips from each of ten customers. From how many customers must she average 80¢ in tips in order to make her overall average in tips 75¢?

27. Eighty tires were sold at $36 each. How many tires must be sold at $60 to have an average selling price of $40 for all the tires sold?

28. If Jennifer had answered six more problems correctly on the test she took, her score would have been 90% instead of 80%. How many problems were on the test?

29. From the sale of their house, the Lees received $26,680, which was the selling price less an 8% commission to the real estate agent. How much was

     a. the selling price of the house?

     b. the real estate agent's commission?

30. The Lees bought another house, agreeing to pay the real estate agent's commission of 8% on the base price. The base price plus the commission came to $37,800. How much was

     a. the base price?

     b. the commission?

31. The costs of two pieces of hospital equipment total $60,000 and are in the ratio
     of 6 to 4. How much does each piece of equipment cost?

32. When a number is divided by five and then three is subtracted, the answer is
     the same as when the number is divided by four and then two is subtracted.
     What is the number?

33. A salesperson has averaged $120 in commissions for each of the past ten days.
     For how many days must her commissions average $160 in order to bring her
     overall average to $150?

34. If Bradley drives twice as fast as Masterson, and if it took Masterson six hours
     to drive 150 km, how long will it take Bradley to drive 400 km?

35. If the length of a rectangle is subtracted from twice its width, the result is
     thirty cm less than the perimeter of the rectangle. What is its length?

36. A man left $144,000 to be divided among his three sons, A, B, and C. How much did each son get if the ratio to be used was, respectively,

   a. 1:1:1?

   b. 12:8:10?

   c. 3:2:1?

37. A bowler averaged a score of 168 for ten games. For how many games must she average 180 to bring her overall average to 172?

38. A bowler averaged a score of 168 for ten games. She bowled enough in the next six games to bring her overall average to 174. What was her average score for the last six games?

39. How much candy selling for $6 a pound is to be mixed with nine pounds of candy selling for $8 a pound to have a mixture selling for $7.50 a pound?

40. Gerry's average score on twelve plays of a computer game was 60,000.

    a. How many games does he have to play at an average score of 80,000 to bring his overall average up to 65,000?

    b. What must his average score be on the next six games in order to bring his overall average up to 65,000?

41. The result of dividing a number by four less than that number is $1\frac{1}{4}$. What are the numbers?

42. The result of dividing a number by three more than that number is $1\frac{3}{4}$. What are the numbers?

43. An investment of $2,000 earned simple interest of $110 one year. What was the rate of interest?

44. Simple interest for two years totaled $329 on a $2,350 investment. What rate of interest was it?

45. The sum of four consecutive integers is 126. What are the integers?

46. Ms. Palmer combined ten pounds of candy selling at $4.00 a pound with twelve pounds of hard candy to make a mixture selling for $5.50 a pound. What was the selling price of the hard candy?

47. Midstate has averaged 1.2 inches of rain for each of the last ten months. For how many months must Midstate average 1.6 inches of rain to bring the overall average rainfall for the period to 1.5 inches?

48. Frank had three-fourths of the problems right on a test. Lucilla had five-sixths of the problems right, which was ten more problems right than Frank.

    a.   How many problems were on the test?

    b.   How many problems did Frank have right?

    c.   How many problems did Lucilla have right?

49. Ignoring air resistance, the number of feet, f, that a dropped object will fall in s seconds is given roughly by the formula f = 16s². Ignore air resistance in this problem.

  a–c. How far will a dropped object fall in

    a. two seconds?

    b. ten seconds?

    c. one minute?

  d–h. To the nearest half-second, how long will an object take to reach the ground if it is dropped from a height of

    d. 100 feet?

    e. 1,454 feet (the height of the roof of the Sears Tower in Chicago)?

    f. 1,250 feet (the height of the roof of the Empire State Building in New York City)?

    g. 984 feet (the height of the Eiffel Tower in Paris)?

    h. $6\frac{1}{2}$ miles (the altitude of a jetliner during a coast-to-coast flight)?

50.   There are twenty-five students in a class. The average of the ten best scores on a test was 94. The average of the ten worst scores was 68. The average of the entire class was 80. What was the average of the other five test scores?

51.   A, B, and C lie on a straight line. C is twice as far from A as A is from B. The distance from B to C, 180 miles, is more than the distance from B to A. How far is it from

    a.   A to B?

    b.   A to C?

52.   The sum of two consecutive multiples of three is 147. What are the numbers?

53.   Five students in a class scored 100 on a test. The average score of the other twenty students in the class was 80. What was the average test score for the class as a whole?

54. If $4,000 is invested at 6%, and $2,000 is invested at a different rate, and if the annual income from these two investments is $420, then what rate does the $2,000 earn?

55. If a store's gross profit is 20% of the selling price, what is the selling price of merchandise costing $75?

56. If a store's markup (amount of profit to be added to cost) is 30% of the cost of merchandise, what is

   a.   the selling price of merchandise costing $60?

   b.   the cost of merchandise selling for $136.50?

57. The average salary in a firm of one hundred employees is $15,000. The salary of ten of the employees is $25,000 each, and the salary of twenty of the employees is $10,000 each. What is the average salary of the remaining employees?

58. Zenobia has eleven nickels and dimes totaling 95¢. How many of each kind of coin has she?

59. Luke is five years older than Marian. The sum of their ages is twenty-seven years. How old is each one?

60. One number is fifteen more than another number. The sum of the two numbers is 69. What are the numbers?

61. Juan is three inches taller than Frances. The sum of their heights is 127 inches. How tall is each one?

62. An eighteen-hole golf course has a total length of 7,256 yards. The total for the last nine holes is more than the total for the first nine by 300 yards. What is the total length of the

    a.   first nine holes?

    b.   last nine holes?

63. The cost of a razor and a package of razor blades was $1.10. The razor was 50¢ more than the blades. How much was each?

64. The cost of a pair of shoes and a pair of boots totaled $18. The shoes cost $4 more than the boots. What was the cost of each pair of footwear?

65. One number is twice as much as another number. The sum of the numbers is 81. What are the numbers?

66. A rectangle is two-thirds as wide as it is long. Its perimeter is 50 cm. What are its dimensions?

67. The junior class has 135 more members than the senior class. The total in the two classes is 835. How many are in each class?

68. Beatrice had ten more problems right than wrong on a 50-problem test. How many problems did she have

    a. right?

    b. wrong?

69. Rose has $2.97 in nickels and pennies. She has three more nickels than pennies. How many of each does she have?

70. A small daily newspaper charges $700 for a full-page ad and $400 for a half-page ad. If ten full-page and half-page ads were sold for $4,600, how many of each were there?

71. The sum of two numbers is 55, and the difference between them is 27. What are the two numbers?

72. A bottle of juice cost 75¢, including the bottle deposit, which was 55¢ less than the cost of the juice alone. How much was

    a. the bottle deposit?

    b. the juice without the bottle deposit?

73. The length of a rectangle is 3 cm more than its width. Its perimeter is 38 cm. What are the rectangle's dimensions?

74. Find two numbers whose sum is 7 and whose difference is 22.

75. Some horses and chickens were in a field. All together, they had one hundred heads and two hundred twenty legs. How many horses were there? How many chickens?

76. Pat bowled a total of 1,187 for six games. Her score for the last three games was 51 more than her score for the first three games. What was her score for

    a.   the first three games?

    b.   the last three games?

77. If the perimeter of an isosceles triangle is 19 cm, and if a leg is 5 cm longer than the base, then how long is

    a.   each leg?

    b.   the base?

78. What number is three more than twice itself?

79. Perry bought an orange and an apple for a total of 40¢. The orange was 10¢ more than the apple. What was the cost of each?

80. Three times one number subtracted from five times another is 25. The sum of the numbers is 37. What are the numbers?

81. The difference between Dinah's age next year and Mario's age last year is ten years. Five years from now, Mario will be twice as old as Dinah will be. How old is each one now?

82. Jet plane A has a ten-person crew. Jet plane B has a six-person crew. On a total of nineteen flights, the crew members of A and B totaled one hundred forty-six. How many flights were made by each plane?

83. A souvenir shop sells tee shirts for $6 and pennants for $3.50. If a total of 50 tee shirts and pennants were sold for $275, how many of each were sold?

84. Anderson bought a fishing license and a hunting license for a total of $18. What was the cost of each if

    a.   the hunting license cost twice as much as the fishing license?

    b.   the hunting license cost $4 more than the fishing license?

    c.   twice the cost of the fishing license was $3 less than the cost of the hunting license?

    d.   the difference between the costs of the two licenses was $10?

85. If twice the width of a rectangle is subtracted from the rectangle's length, the result is two units. The perimeter of the rectangle is sixty-four units. What are the rectangle's dimensions?

86. The units' digit of a two-digit number is three less than the tens' digit. The sum of the digits is eleven. What is the number?

87. Jacobson bought a horse and a cow for a total of $300. What was the cost of each if

    a. the cow cost $50 more than the horse?

    b. the cow cost three times as much as the horse?

    c. the cost of the cow subtracted from twice the cost of the horse was $75?

    d. the difference between the costs of the two was $70?

88. What change takes place in the area of a rectangle if

    a. its length is doubled and its width is tripled?

    b. its length is tripled and its width is doubled?

89. A number of geese and sheep were running a race. If there were a total of one hundred legs and thirty heads, how many of each kind of animal were there?

90. What number is ten more than triple itself?

91. The average score for a class on a test was 84. If three fewer students had taken the test, the average of the remaining students would have had to be 96 in order to have the same overall total for the test.

   a. How many students took the test?

   b. What was the total of all the students' scores?

92. The sum of the digits of a two-digit number is eight. If the digits of the number are reversed and then the result is subtracted from the number, the difference is eighteen. What is the number?

93. A square whose side is half as long as the width of a rectangle can fit exactly eight times into the rectangle. If the area of the rectangle is seventy-two square feet, then

   a. how long is a side of the square?

   b. what are the dimensions of the rectangle?

94. What number is eight more than one-third of itself?

95.   There are thirty students in a general math class. How many boys are there, and
      how many girls are there, if

     a.   there are four more boys than girls?

     b.   there are twice as many girls as boys?

     c.   the number of boys is 25% of the number of girls?

     d.   there are six fewer boys than girls?

96.   The sum of the digits of a two-digit number is fourteen, and the difference
      between the digits is four. What is the number?

97.   In a team bowling match, the first man up and the anchor man bowled a total of
      403. The anchor man's score was 47 more than the first man's score. What was
      each man's score?

98.   The average of two numbers is three-fourths. Their difference is five-sixths.
      What are the numbers?

99. A garment factory sold a number of dresses for a total of $2,040. One-sixth of the dresses were sold for $10 each, one-third for $16 each, and the rest for $20 each. How many dresses were sold at each price, and how much was the total of the sales at each price?

100. Two dozen pens and a ream of paper were purchased for $9. If the ream of paper cost $3 more than a dozen pens, then how much

    a.   was the ream of paper?

    b.   were a dozen pens?

101. Five hundred people watched a basketball game. If there were seventy more people favoring the home team than the visiting team, and if there were fifty who didn't care who won (they just liked basketball games), then how many people favored

    a.   the home team?

    b.   the visiting team?

102. If Garnet were five years older, she would be twice as old as Jeremy, who is two
      years younger than she. How old is each one?

103. A fruit grower sold half of his apples to A and one-third of the remainder to B,
      leaving the fruit grower with 1,000 crates of apples. How many crates of apples

      a. did the fruit grower start with?

      b. were sold to A?

      c. were sold to B?

104. For shoveling snow, Maria changes a nickel a linear foot for a sidewalk, and
      fifteen cents a linear foot for a driveway. If she charged a total of $255 for
      shoveling snow from 2,700 linear feet of sidewalks and driveways in January,
      how many linear feet of snow did she shovel from

      a. sidewalks?

      b. driveways?

105. If Jerry were five years older than he was last year, and if Irene were twice as old as she is now, then the sum of their ages would be forty-eight years. Four years ago, Jerry was two years older than Irene was. How old is each one now?

106. If a three-legged horse is worth twice as much as a two-legged cow, and if the two together are worth $90, then how much is each one worth?

107. Fourteen dresses were sold at a garage sale, some for $4, and the rest for $3. If the total collected for the dresses was $46, how many were sold at each price?

108. Owen bought three pounds of cheese and two loaves of bread for $9.10. A pound of cheese was $1.40 more than a loaf of bread. How much did he pay for

    a.   the cheese he bought?

    b.   the bread he bought?

109. Oranges sell at 20¢ each. Apples sell at 15¢ each. How many of each were sold if

    a. a total of twenty apples and oranges were sold for $3.40?

    b. six more apples than oranges were sold and the total collected was $5.80?

    c. twice as many oranges as apples were sold and the total collected was $9.90?

110. One number is three times as much as another number. Their product is 675. What are the numbers?

111. The sum of the ages of two children is triple the age of one of them. Three years ago, the sum of their ages was four times the age of one of them. How old is each one?

112. A car traveled 100 miles at 40 mph and another 100 miles at 55 mph. What was its average speed for the 200 miles? (Hint: The answer is not $47\frac{1}{2}$ mph.)

113. The sum of two numbers is 81 and their quotient is 8. What are the two
      numbers?

114. Jerry is to add enough water to a liter of 90% sodium hydroxide to make it a
      70% solution. How much water should be added?

115. One number is twice another number. The difference between the numbers is
      thirty-eight. What are the numbers?

116. The value of eighteen dimes and quarters is $2.70. How many of each kind of
      coin are there?

117. Mortimer is five years younger than Loquacia. The difference between the
      squares of their ages is ninety-five. How old is each one?

118. If a number is quadrupled and the result reduced by fifteen, the answer is the
      given number. What is the number?

119. The sum of twice one number and three times another is eighty-nine. The difference between the two numbers is eighteen. What are the numbers?

120. If Zinnia is twice as old as Ulysses and five years younger than Yolanda, how old is each one if

   a. the sum of their ages is thirty-five years?

   b. the sum of Yolanda's and Ulysses' ages is twenty years?

   c. the difference between Zinnia's and Ulysses' ages is eight years?

   d. the difference between Yolanda's and Ulysses' ages is sixteen years?

   e. the sum of Zinnia's and Ulysses' ages is twenty-one years?

   f. the sum of Zinnia's and Yolanda's ages is seventeen years?

   g. Yolanda is thirteen years older than Ulysses?

TEACHING SUGGESTIONS AND DETAILED SOLUTIONS

GENERAL COMMENTS

Problems in each section are arranged in approximately graduated order of difficulty, except that occasionally a relatively easy problem is tossed in among the harder ones just to give the students a pleasant surprise.

Because the objective of this book is to provide word problems with solutions that need only elementary algebra, no problems requiring knowledge of trigonometry have been included, and no problems requiring knowledge of algebra beyond high school algebra have been included. (Some of the harder problems explore an elementary knowledge rather thoroughly, however.)

This section makes comments and suggestions, as well as showing how the answers were obtained.

COMMENTS ABOUT DETAILED SOLUTIONS

When I want to know how an author obtained an answer to a problem, I detest reading something like, "Put x = the number of nickels Alex has, y = the number of...," and so on, and then having to keep referring back to what x and y (and so on) are while I'm trying to relate the equations to the problem. And once I see the equations, I don't need someone to explain how to solve them.

Consequently, I wrote the Detailed Solutions sections the way I'd like to read them. If a problem talks about nickels and dimes, I used n and d as variables. And if it talks about Jan's and Carl's ages, I used J and C as variables. And if it says there were five fewer dogs than cats, I used d

and c as variables, not c and $c - 5$. Because the variables used are so obvious, they are used without explanation.

As another way to eliminate explanations and yet give a clear understanding of how equations were derived from the problem, almost nothing was eliminated between the problem and the equations. For example, if a problem says a radio cost \$10 less than \$100, the equation would show

$$r = 100 - 10.$$

While such a method eliminates wordy explanations, it can also make a solution look more complicated than it is, for when there are several parts (a, b, etc.) to a basic problem, a general system of equations is shown at the start of the Detailed Solution, and then specific values are shown for each part of the problem, rather than rewriting the complete system for each part.

Along that same line, the simplicity of an equation in a Detailed Solution does not necessarily indicate the simplicity of solution from the student's viewpoint. For example, the equations for problem 33 in AGES AND COINS look simpler than many of the systems of equations for problems preceding it. Yet, problem 33 involves fractions (which will automatically terrify some students), whereas none of the preceding problems had equations that used fractions.

In general, then, the difficulty of a problem cannot be accurately judged from seeing how many variables or equations were used in a Detailed Solution.

TEACHING SUGGESTIONS

Students who find word problems difficult are likely to be too discouraged to try very hard to do an assignment of ten problems. Try assigning just two or three problems in order to encourage effort. Once the students experience success with the problems, they will gain confidence, expertise, and speed. Hopefully, they will also learn to enjoy algebra word problems.

Even after the students learn to solve the problems, remember that a problem may be simple for you to solve but baffling to a student. Always do the problems yourself before assigning them to the students, and then figure it will take the students, just to solve the equations after they are set up, at least three to five times as long as it took you.

An explanation that seems obvious and that makes sense to some students may be incomprehensible to others. Try having two or three students explain how they went about solving a problem so that the class sees there are various ways to think about it.

Keep in mind that the equations in the Detailed Solutions sections were written for a clear understanding of how a solution was derived. Where I might have written

$$a + b = 300 - 15$$

here I would write

$$a + b = 285$$

if I were really solving the problem for myself.

Don't expect your students to show picayune steps. You have enough work to do without adding to it by having to play "hunt and find" to try to trace a student's reasoning, so do insist that your students show all (nonpicayune) work in an orderly way. If they can go from

$$3(a + b) = 5a - 7b \text{ to } a = 5b$$

in their heads, it's all right to show the second equation directly under the first. But if they have to do some work on scratch paper to get the second equation, that work should be shown between the two equations.

Also insist that the students check their answers and that they show the work for the check—again, in an orderly way. In this connection, stress that a problem isn't solved unless the answer works for the given conditions, and we can't know an answer works unless we check it out.

Discourage students from writing the number "1" with a top hook (too easily confused with "7") or with a top hook and a bottom cross bar (too time-consuming). Also discourage them from writing a closed "4" (too easily confused with "9" when they write it fast, but the drafting students will give you an argument about it).

Discourage students from using certain variables in their solutions:

(1) As they gain speed and start writing faster,

   (a) a printed "Z" is easily mistaken for a "2." (I use "Z"s, but I make them with crossbars.)

   (b) a written "Z" is easily mistaken for a "3."

   (c) a capital "V" in the same problem with a capital "U" can be mistaken for the "U."

(2) A capital "I" without crossbars is the number "1."

(3) The letter "O" should be avoided as a variable. Without a curl or stem at the top, it is a zero.

(4) The letter "i" should never be used as a variable in a problem that may have imaginary numbers in the solution.

Teach the students not to exchange a capital letter for a small letter. Beginners tend to treat, say, "A" and "a" as the same variable unless they are taught otherwise. Training them correctly from the start saves much trouble later when they run into an equation such as $S = 6s^2$ (The surface area of a cube equals six times the square of one of its sides.)

The above comment applies both to a given formula (if the formula uses a capital, so should the student; if it uses lower case, so should the student) and to the student's choice of a variable for a given problem (whether upper or lower case is chosen, that case should be used consistently throughout).

Since your goal is to teach the students to solve algebra word problems, rather than to give them practice in arithmetic accuracy, encourage them to use hand calculators. Otherwise, some of the problems will be unnecessarily tedious and time-consuming, and the student will stand a good chance of getting bogged down in arithmetic computations and losing sight of what the computations had to do with the solution of the problem.

Allow the students to use as many or as few variables as they like, whatever is the easiest and most natural to them, to solve a problem. (This is not to imply they shouldn't be shown other ways to set up the necessary equations, but neither should they be forced to keep in their heads that $c - 5$ is the number of dogs when they could write $d = c - 5$ and have it staring them in the face if that's what they would rather do.)

If you haven't yet discovered group work, try it for these problems. Separate the class into groups of three to five students to work together in class, and move the classroom desks around so that there are small circles formed for the groups. Choose the students for each group so that some understand better than others how to do the problems, yet so that the best student is not paired with the poorest and so is needlessly held back. (You, too, can work with a small group during this time.)

Depending on the class, you may have to be prepared for some idle chatter the first two or three times you try group work, but once the students find out they have to work during group time, they will make good progress. (Close your classroom door so that the noise doesn't disturb other classes.) The amount of progress from group to group will vary. Change the students around to try to find the best groupings.

HOW TO SOLVE ALGEBRA WORD PROBLEMS

Aside from the fact that the overall approach to solving word problems in this book is different than in most algebra books, there are two things stressed here which may seem relatively minor but which nevertheless make a word problem considerably easier for a student to solve:

(1) Choose the variables for a problem so that they have a natural connection with the problem. (If the problem talks about nickels and dimes, choose n and d, not x and y, as the variables. If it talks about Jerry's age, choose J, not x, as the variable. And so on.)

(2) Insist that your students write complete explanations of the variables chosen, as stressed in Step 1 of Lesson 3 in the Warm Up

section. This will eliminate a large part of many students' troubles with word problems. (Many students write something like "d = dimes" and then have trouble with a problem, not realizing that they don't have a clear idea of what *d* really stands for—e.g., "number of dimes," "total value of all the dimes," "value of one dime.")

Go through each example slowly and carefully with your students. Encourage the students to keep reading the problem in the example as you are going through the solution with them. That is, each example states a problem and then shows how to solve it, but understanding the solution requires that the students keep the problem firmly in mind so that they are able to correlate each statement in the solution with a particular part of the given problem.

Whereas most algebra books assume that students should be taught to solve word problems by using only one variable at first, this book encourages them to use a different variable for each unknown and then to use substitution when necessary. For example, if Bob is 4 years older than Mark, then B = Bob's age, M = Mark's age, and $B = M + 4$, rather than asking the students to remember to write "$M + 4$" every time the problem talks about Bob's age. Because of this, it is suggested that you teach your students to solve simple systems of equations (such as $B = M + 4$; $M + B = 16$) before starting on this book with them.

We know that different methods are needed for different students. One method that seems to work for many students when other methods fail is the "wild guess" method shown in Lesson 7. Consequently, if some of your students have trouble with the problems before that point, don't worry too much about it.

Reassure the students that a surefire method is coming up in Lesson 7, and encourage them to do as much as they can before that time. (This "wild guess" method does work! After using this method on several problems, most students find that they no longer need it, and they automatically write the necessary equations using variables instead of their wild guesses.)

Part of students' troubles with solving word problems lies in their attacking problems haphazardly—doing parts on one sheet and parts on another and then losing track of what they've done and what remains to be done. Insist that your students show all work for each problem, including a clear explanation of each variable. ("And I want the work organized in a logical way! I won't play 'hunt and find' to try to figure out how you got an answer!") Then when a student gets a wrong answer, you or some of the other students will be able to pinpoint the cause of the trouble.

Space limitations have prevented including as many practice problems as are needed for some students to feel comfortable with the lessons taught. It is suggested that you turn to your regular algebra textbook for additional practice problems.

HOW TO SOLVE ALGEBRA WORD PROBLEMS DETAILED SOLUTIONS

Lesson 1
1. $M = J + 5$
2. $T = J + 7$
3. $E = W - 3$
4. $J = R + 2$
5. $I = 2A$
6. $c = p + 60$
7. $B = A + 10$
8. $N = J + 5$
9. $s + l = 54; l = s + 8$
10. $l + s = 47; s = l - 19$

Lesson 2
1. $i = 12f$
2. $m = 12y$
3. $y = \dfrac{m}{12}$
4. $s = 3600h$

5. $c = 100m$

6. $c = \dfrac{o}{24}$

7. $l = \dfrac{m}{1000}$

8. $p = \dfrac{s}{500}$

9. $t = \dfrac{s}{26}$

10. $f = 5280m$

Lesson 3

1. H = Harry's age (in years) now.

M = Mort's age (in years) now.

$H = \dfrac{1}{2}M$ $M = H + 7$

2. J = the no. of marbles June has.
N = the no. of marbles Norm has.
$J = 2N$ $N = J - 9$

3. A = Ann's age (in years) now.
B = Barry's age (in years) now.
C = Cal's age (in years) now.
$A = B + 2$ $B = C - 5$ $C = 2A$

4. M = the amount of money (¢) Mali has.
C = the amount of money (¢) Chet has.

$M = C + 30$ $C = \dfrac{3}{4}M$

5. c = the price ($) per pound of the cheaper candy.
e = the price ($) per pound of the more expensive candy.
$e = c + .90$ $e + c = 5.10$

6. s = the cost (¢) of the soft drink.
d = the cost (¢) of the bottle deposit.
$s = d + 20$ $s + d = 70$

7. T = Terry's age (in years) now.
U = Urania's age (in years) now.
S = Sam's age (in years) now.
$T = 2U$ $U = 3S$ $S = T - 10$
(Notice that we use three variables, even though only one age is asked for.)

8. s = the cost (¢) of the small size.
m = the cost (¢) of the medium size.
l = the cost (¢) of the large size.

$m = s + 40$ $s = \dfrac{1}{3}l$ $l = m + 90$

9. J = the amount of money ($) Jones makes each year now.

$J - 4000 = \dfrac{1}{4}(J + 5000)$

(Notice that this problem is substantially the same as Example 3.3.)

Lesson 4

Note: All answers work in the given problems.

1. The ages are: Harry, 7 years; Mort, 14 years.

2. June has 18, and Norm has 9.

3. The ages are: Ann, 3 years; Barry, 1 year; Cal, 6 years.

4. Chet has 90¢, and Mali has $1.20.

5. The cheaper candy is $2.10 a pound, and the more expensive candy is $3.00 a pound.

6. The bottle deposit is 25¢, and the soft drink is 45¢.

7. Urania is 6 years old. (Sam is 2, and Terry is 12.)

8. The small size is 65¢, the medium size is $1.05, and the large size is $1.95.

9. Jones makes $7000 a year now.

Lesson 5

1. $t + u = 11$; $10u + t = 10t + u - 27$;
$t = 7$; $u = 4$; the given number is 74.

2. $10d + 5n = 160$; $d + 4 = 2n$; $n = 8$;
$d = 12$; he has 12 dimes and 8 nickels.

3. $p + a = 15$; $3.50p + 5a = 15(4)$; $p = 10$;

$a = 5$; 10 pounds of pecans and 5 pounds of almonds should be used.

4. Distance = rate x time; $6 = (b - c)1$; $6 = (b + c)\frac{3}{4}$; $b = 7$; $c = 1$; the boat's speed in still water was 7 mph, and the current's speed was 1 mph.

Lesson 6

1. b = the weight (in pounds) of Brazil nuts to be added; $.75(1 + b) = .9$; $b = .2$; .2 pound of Brazil nuts must be added.

2. **a.** $80(3) = 60f$; $f = 4$. Yes. Peter should sit 4 feet from the center.

   b. Yes. Each should sit the same distance from the center as the other sits.

   c. $50(6) = 40f$; $f = 7\frac{1}{2}$; not unless Perry moves forward or Annette finds something to add weight to her end. (As it is, she needs to sit $7\frac{1}{2}$ feet from the center, but her end of the seesaw is only 6 feet long.)

3. f = the number of rolls of film sold yesterday;
   p = the profit ($) made on each roll of film sold yesterday;
   t = the total profit ($) made on the rolls of film sold yesterday;
   $pf = t$; $(f - 5)(p + .01) = t - 2.80$; $(f + 10)(p - .01) = t + 6.65$; $p = .80$, $f = 125$, $t = 100$; she sold 125 rolls of film at a profit of 80¢ each for a total profit of $100.

4. **a.** $F = aC + b$; $32 = a \cdot 0 + b$; $212 = a \cdot 100 + b$; $a = \frac{9}{5}$, $b = 32$; $F = \frac{9}{5}C + 32$.

b. $F = \frac{9}{5}C + 32$, so $98.6 = \frac{9}{5}C + 32$.

Solving, we get $C = 37$, so the normal temperature of the human body is $37°C$.

c. Using a method analogous to that for part **b** above, we get an answer of $21\frac{1}{9}°C$.

WARM UP

The problems here are designed to build the students' confidence in writing algebraic expressions and in solving simple equations.

Encourage the students to go about solving a problem in whatever way seems the easiest for them. For example, problem 6 says, "Mrs. Ebbing, whose age (in years) is E, is five years younger than her sister. How old is her sister?" It will not occur immediately to all students that if Mrs. Ebbing is younger than her sister, then her sister is older than she, and so her sister's age must be $E + 5$. But the students will readily see that $E = s - 5$ (where s is the sister's age), and they can solve this equation to get $s = E + 5$, the required answer.

Don't rush through these problems. Make sure everyone understands before going from one problem to the next. A little extra time spent at this stage will pay dividends in time saved when the students start doing the problems in the other sections.

Your students might find it helpful to go through some of the problems in the WARM-UP section in this book before doing the problems here.

Practice some basic expressions with your students: If J = Joe's age (in years) now, then

1. Joe's age a year ago is $J - 1$.

2. Joe's age five years from now is J + 5.

3. twice Joe's age is 2J.

4. twice Joe's age a year ago is
    2(J - 1), not 2J - 1.

And so on.

Similarly, practice some basic equations with your students. If J = Joe's age (in years) now, and s = his sister's age (in years) now, then

1. J - 1 = s says that Joe's age last year is his sister's age this year.

2. J - 1 = 2(s - 1) says that last year Joe was twice as old as his sister was.

3. J - 1 = 2s - 1 says that last year Joe was one year younger than twice the age of his sister now.

4. $J + 10 = \frac{3}{2} J$ says that ten years

    from now Joe will be one and a half times as old as he is now.

And so on.

Because decimals are harder to work with than whole numbers, the equations shown in this answer section for coin problems use whole numbers. It is understood, however, that if a problem says nickels and dimes have a total value of $1.60 and the equation shown here is

$$5n + 10d = 160,$$

the student may have chosen to show the equation as

$$.05n + .10d = 1.60$$
(But not as 5n + 10d = 1.60.)

When your students have done a few problems, ask them why money signs aren't used in setting up the equations. [Why not (5¢)n + (10¢)d = 160¢? Why not $.05n + $.10d = $1.60?] We can probably

take our choice of any of the following answers:

1. The signs don't contribute to the solution, and

    a. they make the equation look more complicated than need be.

    b. we are too lazy to write them when they don't do any good.

2. The mathematics involved does not depend on arbitrary units of measurement—dollars, cents, miles, feet, whatever.

For example,

(5 miles)n + (10 miles)d = 160 miles is exactly the same mathematically as

$$(5¢)n + (10¢)d = 160¢.$$

Thus, such units of measurement may be omitted without affecting the mathematics of the equation.

3. Both sides of any equation may be divided by the same nonzero number without changing the truth value of the equation. So if we started out by including the units in an equation, we could divide both sides by one unit (1¢ or 1 mile or $1 or whatever) and eliminate such units. Since we could do this, there is no point in including them in the first place.

All of these reasons boil down to the same thing: the units aren't needed. And they not only aren't helpful but they are downright distracting. So we simply exclude them.

Despite the foregoing discussion, you may find it helpful to insist that some students use appropriate money signs if you find that their initial equations tend to mix units. Referring back to the example given above, 5n + 10d = 160, a student who writes

$$5n + 10d = 1.60$$

is using mixed units, and such a student might benefit from being forced to write

$$(5¢)n + (10¢)d = \$1.60,$$

thus making it obvious that the equation would have to be divided by 1¢ on the left but $1 on the right in order to have 5n + 10d = 1.60. (Or, in the students' parlance, you can't cancel ¢ with $ in an equation, so the equation must be wrong.)

You might like to point out to your students that their work will be simplified if they can divide both sides of an initial equation by a common factor before proceeding with the solution. For instance, the system

$$5n + 10d = 160$$
$$n + d = 20$$

becomes simpler to work with if both sides of the first equation are divided by 5:

$$n + 2d = 32$$
$$n + d = 20.$$

When checking a solution, however, make sure the student checks by using the original set of equations, since it is possible that the solution works for the simplified set but that the student made an error in simplifying an original equation. For example, suppose the student, using the set

$$5n + 10d = 160$$

$$n + d = 20$$

comes up with the simplified set

$$n + 2d = 33$$

$$n + d = 20.$$

Then the student's solution (n = 7, d = 13) would check out in the simplified set but not in the original set.

DETAILED SOLUTIONS FOR WARM UP

AGES

1. $J - 1$.

2. $A - 12$

3. $S - \dfrac{6}{12}$ OR $S - \dfrac{1}{2}$

4. $B - 24$

5. $s - 5$

6. $E + 5$

7. $\dfrac{F}{2}$; $F - 10$

8. $C + \dfrac{8}{12}$ or $C + \dfrac{2}{3}$

9. $B + 1$

10. $J - 10$

11. $J - 13$

12. $\dfrac{y}{2} + 3$

13. **a.** $B - 5$; **b.** $\dfrac{B + 3}{2} - 3$
    c. $B + 11$

14. **a.** $A + B + C$
    b. $2(A + B + C) + 10$
    c. $2(A + B + C) + 15$

15. $S - 8$; $S - 5$

16. **a.** $\dfrac{M}{2}$; $3M$; **b.** $2P$; $6P$
    c. $\dfrac{R}{3}$; $\dfrac{R}{6}$

17. $K + 8$

18. a. $A = B - 4$

 b. $B + 5 = 2(B - 3)$

 c. $C = \dfrac{1}{2}(A + B)$

 d. $B + 5 = A + C$

 e. $B - 5 = A - 1$

 f. $C = \dfrac{3}{2}(B - 5)$

 g. $B + C = 3A - 1$

 h. $C + 9 = 2C$

 i. $B + 1 = C + 3$

 j. $B - 2 = A + 2$

 k. $2B + 3C = 7A$

 l. $2B + 3C = A^2$

 m. $2(C - 4) = B - 1$

 n. $B - 10 + A + 1 = C$

 o. $B^2 - C^2 = 2(B + C)$

 p. $\dfrac{A}{2} + \dfrac{C}{3} = \dfrac{B}{2} + 1$

COINS

19. a. $5n$ cents; **b.** $25q$ cents

 c. $(5n + 25q)$ cents

20. $(5n - p)$ cents

21. $q = d + 5$, so the amount in cents is

 a. $10(q - 5) + 25q$

 b. $10d + 25(d + 5)$

22. $p = 2n$, so the amount in cents is

 a. $p + 5\left(\dfrac{p}{2}\right)$; **b.** $2n + 5n$

23. $q = 2d$, so the amount in cents is

 a. $10d + 25(2d)$

 b. $10\left(\dfrac{q}{2}\right) + 25q$

24. $q = d - 5$, so the amount in cents is
 a. $10d + 25(d - 5)$
 b. $10(q + 5) + 25q$

25. $d = 2q$, and $n = d + 5$, so the amount in cents is

 a. $5n + 10(n - 5) + 25\left(\dfrac{n - 5}{2}\right)$

 b. $5(d + 5) + 10d + 25\left(\dfrac{d}{2}\right)$

 c. $5(2q + 5) + 10(2q) + 25q$

26. $2(p - 5) = d$, so she has $\{p + 10[2(p - 5)]\}$ cents

27. a. $10(d - 2) = 25(q - 3)$

 b. $25q = 5n + 75$

 c. $5n = 10d - 20$

 d. $25(q + 1) = 3(5n)$

 e. $p + 5n + 10d = 25q + 3$

 f. $5(n + 5) + 10(d - 2) = 25q$

 g. $p + d = n + q$

 h. $25(q + 1) = 5n + 100$

 i. $p + 17 + 5n + 10(d-2) = 25q$

 j. $5(3n) + 10(2d) = 5n + 10d + 170$ OR $.05(3n) + .10(2d) = .05n + .10d + 1.70$

 k. $10d + 25q = 5n + 145$ OR $.10d + .25q = .05n + 1.45$

 l. $10(d + 3) = 2(5n)$

 m. $2(5n + 10d) = 25q + 115$ OR $2(.05n + .10d) = .25q + 1.15$

 n. $5p = 5(n - 2)$

o. $\dfrac{p + 5(n-1) + 10d + 25q}{2} = 25q - 1$

p. $10d = 9p - 2$

MEASUREMENTS

28. a. $f = 3y$ **b.** $m = 60h$

c. $d = 7w$ **d.** $c = 100m$

e. $h = 24$ **f.** $f = 5280m$

g. $w = 52y$ OR $w = (52\tfrac{1}{7})y$

h. $s = 3600h$ **i.** $m = sh$

j. $o = 16p$

29. a. $w(w + 3)$ **b.** $l(l - 3)$

30. a. $d = rt$ **b.** $r = \dfrac{d}{t}$ **c.** $t = \dfrac{d}{r}$

31. a. $h - 2$ **b.** $h + 5$

c. $h + \dfrac{1}{2}$ **d.** $h - \dfrac{1}{4}$ **e.** $h + \dfrac{23}{60}$

32. $d = kh$, so
$kh = (k + 20)(h - 3)$

33. $d = rt$, so

$rt = (r + 5)(t - \dfrac{10}{60})$

34. a. $p - c$ **b.** $p + c$

35. $r - c$

36. a. $s + c$ **b.** $s - c$

37. a. $3d$ minutes slow

b. It would take 20 days to be 1 hour slow, so it would take 20 x 12, or 240, days to be 12 hours slow and so show the correct

time again. (Not an algebra problem, but fun all the same. Or, if we insist, $\dfrac{3d}{60} = 12$, so d =240.)

38. a. $(w - 2)l$ **b.** $w(l + 3)$
   c. $(w - 2)(l + 4)$
   d. $(w + \dfrac{1}{2})l$ **e.** $w(l - \dfrac{7}{12})$

39. a. $4p$ dollars

   b. $(2\tfrac{6}{8})p$ dollars

40. a. $(t + b)$ kph

   b. time = $\dfrac{\text{distance}}{\text{rate}}$, so (letting d = distance in kilometers) the answer is $\dfrac{d}{t + b}$ hours.

41. a. $\dfrac{32q}{9}$ **b.** $\dfrac{2(32)h}{9}$

42. a. $4q;$ **b.** $5(4q)$

43. a. $h_1 m_1 + h_2 m_2$

   b. $h_1(m_1 + 3) + h_2 m_2$

44. $16.25(\dfrac{wl}{9})$

45. a. s^3

   b. $(12s)^3$ or $1728s^3$

   c. $(s - 2)^3$

   d. $(12s - 24)^3$ OR $1728(s - 2)^3$

   e. $(s - \dfrac{1}{12})^3$

   f. $(12s - 1)^3$ OR $1728(s - \dfrac{1}{12})^3$

46. $r = \dfrac{d}{2}$, so

i. $3(100h + 10t + u) + 1$ OR

$300h + 30t + 3u + 1$

a. $\pi\left(\dfrac{d+2}{2}\right)^2$ OR $\pi(r+1)^2$

49. 1, 3, 9, 11, 33, and 99

b. $\pi\left(\dfrac{d-\frac{1}{2}}{2}\right)^2$ OR $\pi(r-\frac{1}{4})^2$

50. a. $\dfrac{n}{d}$ **b.** $\dfrac{n+2}{d}$ **c.** $\dfrac{d}{n}$

c. $\pi\left(\dfrac{d-\frac{7}{12}}{2}\right)^2$ OR $\pi(r-\frac{7}{24})^2$

d. $\dfrac{n}{d}+\dfrac{d}{n}$ **e.** $\dfrac{n-3}{d+5}$

NUMBERS

f. $\dfrac{n-3}{d+5}+6$ **g.** $3(\dfrac{n}{d}+\dfrac{d}{n})$

47. a. $10t + u$

WORK RATES

b. $10t + u + 3$

c. $10t + u + 15$ [OR $10(t+1) + (u+$ 5), but this could be misleading if the student thinks $t+1$ or $u+5$ is necessarily a one-digit number]

51. a. $\dfrac{1}{P}$ **b.** $\dfrac{1}{R}$

c. $\dfrac{1}{P}+\dfrac{1}{R}$ **d.** $\dfrac{h}{P}$

d. $10u + t$ **e.** $t + u$ **f.** tu

g. $2(10t + u)$ OR $20t + 2u$

e. $\dfrac{h}{P}+\dfrac{h}{R}$ OR $h(\dfrac{1}{P}+\dfrac{1}{R})$

h. $\dfrac{1}{2}(10t + u) - 5$

f. $\dfrac{h}{P}+\dfrac{h-2}{R}$ **g.** $\dfrac{4}{P}+\dfrac{h-4}{R}$

48. a. $100h + 10t + u$

52. a. $\dfrac{m}{A}+\dfrac{m}{B}$

b. $100u + 10t + h$

b. $\dfrac{m}{A}-\dfrac{m}{C}$

c. $2(100u + 10t + h)$ OR

$200u + 20t + 2h$

c. $\dfrac{m}{A}+\dfrac{m}{B}-\dfrac{m}{C}$

d. $101h + 20t + 101u$

d. $\dfrac{10+m}{A}+\dfrac{m}{B}-\dfrac{m}{C}$

e. $99h - 99u$ OR $99u - 99h$

e. $\dfrac{2}{3}\cdot\dfrac{m}{B}$, not $\dfrac{M}{\frac{2}{3}B}$, which would be

f. $99h - 99u$ **g.** $99u - 99h$

$\dfrac{3}{2}\cdot\dfrac{m}{B}$

h. $100h + 10t + u + 500$ OR

$100(h + 5) + 10t + u$

f. $\dfrac{10}{A}-\dfrac{10}{C}+\dfrac{m-10}{A}$ $+\dfrac{m-10}{B}$ OR

$\dfrac{m}{A}+\dfrac{m-10}{B}$ $-\dfrac{10}{C}$

55. a. $\$4(3) + \$2.50p$

b. $4m + \$2.50p$

c. $a = \dfrac{\$4(3) + \$2.50p}{3 + p}$

d. $a = \dfrac{\$4m + \$2.50p}{m + p}$

e. $a = \dfrac{\$4m + \$2.50(10 - m)}{10}$

f. $3 = \dfrac{4m + 2.50(10 - m)}{10}$ OR

   $3 = \dfrac{4(10 - p) + 2.50p}{10}$

g. $3 = \dfrac{4m + 2.50(t - m)}{t}$ OR

   $3 = \dfrac{4(t - p) + 2.50p}{t}$

h. $d = \dfrac{4m + 2.50(t - m)}{t}$ OR

   $d = \dfrac{4(t - p) + 2.50p}{t}$

INTEREST

56. $\dfrac{\$5000r + \$3000b}{100}$

57. $\dfrac{r}{4}\%$

58. **a.** $\left(\dfrac{\$6d + \$2000r}{100} \right)$

   b. $\dfrac{1}{4}\left(\dfrac{\$6d + \$2000r}{100} \right)$

59. **a.** $\dfrac{\$6000r + \$4000b}{100}$

b. $\dfrac{\$sr + \$(10{,}000 - s)b}{100}$

60. **a.** .09;   **b.** .045

   c. .0225;   **d.** .0075

   e. 3;   **f.** 6

   g. 12;   **h.** 36

61. **a.** $A = \$2000(1.08)^2$

   b. $A = \$2000(1.02)^8$

   c. $A = \$2000(1.06)^5$

   d. $A = \$2000(1.005)^{60}$

62. **a.** $P = \dfrac{\$5000}{1.02^{20}}$

   b. $\dfrac{\$7{,}450.85}{1.05^{16}}$

63. **a.** $A = \$500(1.015)^2$

   b. $A = \$500(1.015)^{12}$

MISCELLANEOUS

64. **a.** $G = rh$

   b. $G = 40r + (h - 40)\dfrac{3r}{2}$

   c. $G = 40r + 10(\dfrac{3}{2}r) + 5(2r)$

   d. $G = 30r + t(\dfrac{3}{2}r) + (h - 30 - t)(2r)$

65. $\dfrac{6f + 6g}{12}$ OR $\dfrac{f + g}{2}$

66. $\dfrac{3f + 3g + 2h + 4k}{12}$

67. $.75s + .70k$

68. a. $\dfrac{5a + n}{6}$

   b. $6b - 5a$

69. a. $t = pc$ dollars

   b. $t = (p - 5)(c + 3)$ dollars

70. $\dfrac{N}{.65}$

71. $dc = (d - 3)(c + 5)$

AGES AND COINS

Your students might find it helpful to go through some of the problems in the WARM UP section before doing the problems here.

Practice some basic expressions with your students: If J = Joe's age (in years) now, then

  1. Joe's age a year ago is $J - 1$.

  2. Joe's age five years from now is $J + 5$.

  3. twice Joe's age is $2J$.

  4. twice Joe's age a year ago is $2(J - 1)$, not $2J - 1$.

And so on. Similarly, practice some basic equations with your students. If J = Joe's age (in years) now, and s = his sister's age (in years) now, then

  1. $J - 1 = s$ says that Joe's age last year is his sister's age this year.

  2. $J - 1 = 2(s - 1)$ says that last year Joe was twice as old as his sister was.

  3. $J - 1 = 2s - 1$ says that last year Joe was one year younger than twice the age of his sister now.

4. $J + 10 = \dfrac{3}{2}\,J$ says that ten years from now Joe will be one and a half times as old as he is now.

And so on. Because decimals are harder to work with than whole numbers, the equations shown in this Teacher's Manual for coin problems use whole numbers. It is understood, however, that if a problem says nickels and dimes have a total value of $1.60 and the equation shown here is

$$5n + 10d = 160,$$

the student may have chosen to show the equation as

$$.05n + .10d = 1.60.$$

(But not as $5n + 10d = 1.60$.)

When your students have done a few problems, ask them why money signs aren't used in setting up the equations. [Why not $(5¢)n + (10¢)d = 160¢$? Why not $\$.05n + \$.10d = \$1.60$?] We can probably take our choice of any of the following answers:

  1. The signs don't contribute to the solution, and
     a. they make the equation look more complicated than need be.

     b. we are too lazy to write them when they don't do any good.

  2. The mathematics involved does not depend on arbitrary units of measurement—dollars, cents, miles, feet, whatever. For example,

$$(5 \text{ miles})n + (10 \text{ miles})d = 160 \text{ miles}$$

is exactly the same mathematically as

$$(5¢)n + (10¢)d = 160¢.$$

Thus, such units of measurement may be omitted without affecting the mathematics of the equation.

3. Both sides of any equation may be divided by the same nonzero number without changing the truth value of the equation. So if we started out by including the units in an equation, we could divide both sides by one unit (1¢ or 1 mile or $1 or whatever) and eliminate such units. Since we could do this, there is no point in including them in the first place.

All of these reasons boil down to the same thing: the units aren't needed. And they not only aren't helpful but they are downright distracting. So we simply exclude them.

Despite the foregoing discussion, you may find it helpful to insist that some students use appropriate money signs if you find that their initial equations tend to mix units. Referring back to the example given above, $5n + 10d = 160$, a student who writes

$$5n + 10d = 1.60$$

is using mixed units, and such a student might benefit from being forced to write

$$(5¢)n + (10¢)d = \$1.60,$$

thus making it obvious that the equation would have to be divided by 1¢ on the left but $1 on the right in order to have $5n + 10d = 1.60$. (Or, in the students' parlance, you can't cancel ¢ with $ in an equation, so the equation must be wrong.)

You might like to point out to your students that their work will be simplified if they can divide both sides of an initial equation by a common factor before proceeding with the solution. For instance, the system

$$5n + 10d = 160$$
$$n + d = 20$$

becomes simpler to work with if both sides of the first equation are divided by 5:

$$n + 2d = 32$$
$$n + d = 20.$$

When checking a solution, however, make sure the student checks by using the original set of equations, since it is possible that the solution works for the simplified set but that the student made an error in simplifying an original equation. For example, suppose the student, using the set

$$5n + 10d = 160$$
$$n + d = 20$$

comes up with the simplified set

$$n + 2d = 33$$
$$n + d = 20.$$

Then the student's solution ($n = 7$, $d = 13$) would check out in the simplified set but not in the original set.

AGES AND COINS DETAILED SOLUTIONS

(AGES)

1. 6. $3C + 10 = 5C - 2$

2. 15. $3(A - 5) = 2A$

3. $G = 15$; $V = 8$
$G + V = 23$
$G = V + 7$

4. $B = 13$; $L = 18$
$B = L - 5$
$B + L = 31$

5. $H = 8$; $J = 16$
$J + H = 24$
$J = 2H$

6. $E = 11;\ F = 8$
$E + 5 = 2F$
$E - 3 = F$

7. 8. $2L + 5 = 3(L - 1)$

8. $K = 18;\ L = 10$
$K + 2 = 2L$
$L = K - 8$

9. $E = 11;\ F = 8$
$E = F + 3$
$E + F = 19$

10. $H = 8;\ I = 10$
$H + I = 18$
$H = I - 2$

11. $M = 17;\ P = 11$
$M = P + 6$
$M + P = 28$

12. 11. $2(D - 2) = 3(D - 5)$

13. $A = 15;\ J = 24$
$J = 2(A - 3)$
$J + A = 39$

14. 21. $2(S - 5) + 3 = S + 14$

15. $J = 10;\ s = 15$
$3J = 2s$
$s = J + 5$

16. $E = 11;\ P = 17$
$P - 9 = 4(E - 9)$
$P + 5 = 2E$

17. $A = 15;\ B = 17$
$3A = 2B + 11$
$A + B = 2B - 2$

18. $M = 10;\ J = 18$
$J = M - 2 + 10$
$J - 2 = 2(M - 2)$

19. $W = 14;\ X = 6$
$W = X + 8$
$W + 2 = 2(X + 2)$

20.
    a. $A = 15;\ B = 12$
       $A - B = 3$
       $A + B = 27$

    b. $A = 12;\ B = 15$
       $B - A = 3$
       $B + A = 27$

21. 6. $17 = 5 + 2K$

22. $M = 12;\ N = 17$
$M + 2 = N - 3$
$M + N = 29$

23. $A = 12;\ B = 15$
$5A - 3B = B$
$A + B = 27$

24. $J = 14;\ M = 28$
$M - 7 = 3(J - 7)$
$M = 2J$

25. $C = 14;\ N = 20$
$N = 2(C - 4)$
$N + C = 34$

26. $S = 11;\ T = 8$
$S + 5 = 2T$
$T = S - 3$

27.
    a. 3. $9 + D = 2(9 - D)$

    b. 27. $9 + D = 2(D - 9)$

28. 17; 7
$D + b = 24$
$D - b = 10$ or $b - D = 10$

29. $E = 17;\ L = 15;\ Z = 3$
$E = L + 2$
$L = 5Z$
$L + 1 = 4(Z + 1)$

30. $A = 4;\ Y = 10;\ Z = 8$
$Y = Z + 2$
$Z = A + 4$
$A + Y + Z = 22$

31. **a.** 13 **b.** 9
$C = D + 4$
$2C + C + D = 48$

32. $C = 11; M = 13$
$C + 5 = 2(M - 5)$
$M + 5 = 3(C - 5)$

33. $2E = \frac{1}{2}F$

   a. 3. $2E = \frac{1}{2}(12)$

   b. 10. $2(2\frac{1}{2}) = \frac{1}{2}F$

34. $H = 11; b = 3$
$H + 5 = 2(b + 5)$
$b = H - 8$

35. $C = 3; D = 4$
$C + 5 = 2D$
$D + 5 = 3C$

36. $E = 10; A = 30; B = 15$
$A = 3E$
$A = 2B$
$E = B - 5$

37. $P = 5; S = 2$
$P + 1 = 2(S + 1)$
$S = P - 3$

38. $M = 9; N = 1$
$M + 3 = 2(N + 3) + 4$
$N = M - 8$

39. $U = 23; V = 11$
$U - 5 = 3(V - 5)$
$U + 1 = 2(V + 1)$

40. **a.** 16; **b.** 48 **c.** 43
$M = H - 5$
$H = 3J$
$M + H + J = 107$

41. **a.** 8; **b.** 6 **c.** 2
$J = 2(H - 2)$
$H = 3Y$
$Y = J - 6$

42. 5. $A = \frac{1}{2}(A + 5)$

43. 8. $B - 2 = \frac{1}{2}(B + 4)$

44. 8. $F + 1 = \frac{1}{2}(F + 10)$

45. $R = 6; M = 26$

$R + 7 = \frac{1}{2}M$

$M = 4R + 2$

46. $P = 3; R = 7$

$P - 1 = \frac{1}{3}(R - 1)$

$P + 1 = \frac{1}{2}(R + 1)$

47. 16. $\frac{1}{2}D = D - 3 - 5$

48. $B = 7; T = 21$
$T + 7 = 2(B + 7)$

$B = \frac{1}{3}T$

49. 10. $\frac{1}{3}(S + 5) = \frac{1}{2}S$

50. 10. $\frac{1}{2}L + 20 = \frac{5}{2}L$

51. $Q = 16; S = 4$

$\frac{1}{2}Q = 2s$

$s = Q - 12$

52. $E = 18; J = 10$

$J - 2 = \frac{1}{2}(E - 2)$

$J + E = 28$

53. 12. $D = \frac{1}{2}[3(D - 4)]$

54. 16. $\frac{1}{2}(3W) = 2(W - 4)$

55. $E = 5$; $J = 19$

$\frac{1}{2}(J + 5) = 3(E - 1)$

$(J + 1) + (E + 1) = 26$

56. $G = 5$; $H = 13$

$G - 1 = \frac{1}{3}(H - 1)$

$H + 3 = 2(G + 3)$

57. 3. $\frac{1}{3}G = \frac{1}{2}(G - 1)$

58. 6. $K - 2 = \frac{1}{3}(2K)$

59. 6. $3M - 8 = 2(M - 1)$

60. a. 12 **b.** 10 **c.** 3

$L = H + 2$

$H = M + 7$

$M = \frac{1}{4}L$

61. $D = 12$; $S_1 = 6$ $S_2 = 8$

$D + s_1 + s_2 = 26$

$D = 2s_1$

$D = \frac{3}{2}s_2$

62. $C + D - E = 2D + 3$

$C + E - D = 2C - 7$

a. 2

b. Chester is five years older than Elwood.

63. 10. $K = 2(\frac{1}{5}K + 3)$

64. 12. $\frac{1}{2}(E + 2) = \frac{1}{3}E + 3$

65. $B = 12$; $E = 6$; $G = 8$

$B = 2E$

$B = \frac{3}{2}G$

$B + E + G = 26$

(COINS)

66. a. $11n, 4d$

$n + d = 15$

$n = d + 7$

b. 95¢

$11(5¢) + 4(10¢)$

67. a. $8d, 6q$

$q = d - 2$

$q + d = 14$

b. $2.30

$8(\$.10) + 6(\$.25)$

68. a. $5n, 12d$

$n + d = 17$

$5n + 10d = 145$

b. $16n, 1d$

$n + d = 17$

$5n + 10d = 90$

69. $52n, 45d$

$n + d = 97$

$5n + 10d = 710$

70. a. $8n, 4d$

$n = 2d$

$5n + 10d = 80$

b. $12n, 6d$

$n = 2d$

$5n + 10d = 120$

71. a. $24d; 12q$

$d = 2q$

$d - 5 = q + 7$

b. $5.40

$24(\$.10) + 12(\$.25)$

72. a. $10n, 3d$

$n = d + 7$
$5n + 10d = 80$

b. $9n, 2d$
$n = d + 7$
$5n + 10d = 65$

c. $14n, 7d$
$n = d + 7$
$5n + 10d = 140$

73.a–f. $5n + 10d = 500$

a. $40n, 30d$
$n = d + 10$

b. $28n, 36d$
$d = n + 8$

c. $80n, 10d$
$5n = 4(10d)$

d. $20n, 40d$
$10d = 4(5n)$

e. $50n, 25d$
$n = 2d$

f. $20n, 40d$
$d = 2n$

74. a. $22n, 15d$
$n + d = 37$
$10d = 5n + 40$

b. 2.60
$22(\$.05) + 15(\$.10)$

75. a. $4n, 7d$
$n + d = 11$
$5n + 10d = 90$

b. $19n, 21d$
$n + d = 40$
$d = n + 2$

c. 3.05
$19(\$.05) + 21(\$.10)$

d. $23n, 28d$
Add answers a and b.

e. 3.95
$23(\$.05) + 28(\$.10)$

76. $31n, 23d$
$n + d = 54$
$5(n + 3) + 10d = 400$ or
$5n + 10d = 400 - 15$

77. 12. $5x - 10x = -60$

78. $13n, 11d, 6q$
$n = d + 2$
$d = q + 5$
$5n + 10d + 25q = 325$

79. a. $30\,p, 6n, 2d$
$n = 3d$
$p = 5n$
$p + n + d = 38$

b. $80¢$
$30(1¢) + 6(5¢) + 2(10¢)$

c. $105p, 21n, 7d$
$n = 3d$
$p = 5n$
$p + 5n + 10d = 280$

80. a. $36n, 33d, 31q$
$n - 5 = d - 2 = q$
$5n + 10d + 25q = 1285$

b. $53n, 50d, 48q$
$n - 5 = d - 2 = q$
$n + d + q = 151$

c. 19.65
$53(\$.05) + 50(\$.10) + 48(\$.25)$

81. a. Since Craig has 20¢ more in nickels, Dennis must have 20¢ more in dimes. So Dennis has two more dimes than Craig has.

b. 55. From part a, it follows that Dennis has two fewer coins than Craig.

c–d. $\dfrac{\$8.70}{2} = \$4.35$ for each boy, so

$n + d = 57$
$5n + 10d = 435$

c. $27n, 30d$

d. $23n, 32d$
Either use the same method as
for part *c* or reason as follows:
Dennis has four fewer nickels
(given) and two more dimes (from
part a) than Craig. Use this
answer along with the the answer
to part c.

82. a. $10n, 7d, 5q$
$25q = 5n + 75$
$5n = 10d - 20$
$25(q + 1) = 3(5n)$

b. $2.45
$10(\$.05) + 7(\$.10) + 5(\$.25)$

83. $5d, 5q$
$d + q = 10$
$25(q - 3) + 10(d - 2) + 15 =$

$\frac{1}{2}(25q + 10d + 15)$

84. a–c. $n + d + q = 135$
$5n + 10d + 25q = 2350$
$q = 3n$

a. 25, $1.25
$25(\$.05)$

b. 35, $3.50
$35(\$.10)$

c. 75, $18.75
$75(\$.25)$

85. $5d, 7q$
Let *d* and *q* be the numbers of
dimes and quarters Lucille has. Then
when the numbers of coins are
reversed, *d* becomes the number of
quarters, and *q* becomes the number
of dimes.

$10d + 25q = 225$
$10q + 25d = 225 - 30$

86. a. $11n, 10d, 13q$
$5n + 10d = 155$
$10d + 25q = 425$
$5n + 25q = 380$

b. $4.80
$11(\$.05) + 10(\$.10) + 13(\$.25)$ OR,
since everything was added twice,

$$\frac{\$1.55 + \$4.25 + \$3.80}{2}$$

87. a. $300n, 200d$
$10d = 5n + 500$
$d = \frac{2}{3}n$

b. $15 *n*, $20 *d*, $35 total
$300(\$.05); 200(\$.10); \$15 + \$20$

88. $3n, 18d, 9q$

$d = 2q$

$n = \frac{1}{3}q$

$5n + 10d + 25q = 420$

89. $12n, 16d, 32q$
$5n + 10d + 25q = 1020$
$q = 2d$
$d = n + 4$

90. a. $2p, 7n, 8d$
$p + 5n + 10d = 117$
$d = 4p$
$n = p + 5$

b. $7p, 2n, 8d$
$p + 5n + 10d = 97$
$d = p + 1$
$n = p - 5$

c. 15 of each
$p + 5n + 10d = 240$
$p = n = d$

d. 60 p, 30n, 15d
$p + 5n + 10d = 360$
$p = 2n$
$n = 2d$

e. 18p, 9n, 13d

$p + 5n + 10d = 193$

$d = \dfrac{1}{2}(n + p) - \dfrac{1}{2}$

$n = \dfrac{1}{2}p$

91. 25p, 18n, 22d
$d = n + 4$
$n = p - 7$
$p + 5n + 10d = 335$

92. 10n, 5d, 10q

$q = 2d$

$d = \dfrac{1}{2}n$

$5n + 10d + 25q = 350$

93. a. 24n, 48d, 16q
$25q = 5n + 280$
$n = \dfrac{1}{2}d$
$10d = 25q + 80$

b. nickels, \$1.20; dimes, \$4.80;
quarters, \$4.00
\$.05(24); \$.10(48); \$.25(16)

c. \$10.00
\$1.20 + \$4.80 + \$4.00

94. 15p, 19n, 19d, 5q
$n + d = p + q + 18$
$p = 3q$
$n = d$
$p + 5n + 10d + 25q = 425$

95. a. \$1.50. $2m - \dfrac{1}{3}m = \$2.50$

b. 50¢. $\dfrac{1}{3}(150¢)$

c. 5d, 4q
$10d + 25q = 150$
$d + q = 9$
Or part c can be solved without
using part b:

$2(10d + 25q) - \dfrac{1}{3}(10d + 25q) = 250$

$d + q = 9$

96. a. 21n, 24d
$(n + 5)5 + 2(n + 5)10 =$
$5n + 10d + 305$
$d = n + 3$

b. \$3.45
21(\$.05) + 24(\$.10)

97. 5n, 11d, 14q
$5n + 10d + 25q = 485$
$5d + 10n + 25q = 455$
$q = d + 3$

(For an explanation of the second
equation in 97 see the note above
about the solution of problem 85.)

98. 188p, 115n, 230d, 235q
$p + 5n + 10d + 25q = 8938$
$q = d + 5$
$d = 2n$
$p = n + 73$

99. a. 8n, 8q

$2n(5) + \dfrac{1}{2}q(25) = 5n + 25q - 60$

$n + q = 16$

b. \$2.40.
8(\$.05) + 8(\$.25)

c. 3n, 6q

$5n + 25q = 165$

$2(5n) + \dfrac{1}{2}(25q) = 165 - 60$

100. a. 30d, 40q
$\dfrac{3}{2}q + \dfrac{1}{3}d = q + d$

$\frac{1}{2}q(25) - \frac{2}{3}d(10) = 300$

The second equation could also

be $\frac{3}{2}q(25) + \frac{1}{3}d(10) =$

$25q + 10d + 300.$

b. $13
30($.10) + 40($.25)

101. a. $3p, 5n, 7d, 98¢$
$p + n + d = 15$
$d = n + 2$
$n = p + 2$
$3(1¢) + 5(5¢) + 7(10¢)$

b. $87p, 13n, 25d, \$4.02$

$p + n + d = 125$

$d = \frac{1}{4}(n + p)$

$n = \frac{1}{8}(p + d) - 1$

$87($.01) + 13($.05) + 25($.10)$

c. $14p, 35n, 7d, \$2.59$

$p + n + d = 56$

$d = \frac{1}{5}n$

$n = \frac{5}{2}p$

$14($.01) + 35($.05) + 7($.10)$

d. $64p, 8n, 4d, \$1.44$

$p + n + d = 76$

$n = \frac{1}{8}p$

$d = n - 4$

$64($.01) + 8($.05) + 4($.10)$

e. $15p, 10n, 5d, \$1.15$

$p + n + d = 30$

$n = 2d$

$n = \frac{2}{3}p$

$15($.01) + 10($.05) + 5($.10)$

102. a. $10d, 3q$

$\frac{3}{2}d + \frac{1}{3}q = d + q + 3$

$\frac{3}{2}d(10) + \frac{1}{3}q(25) = 10d + 25q$

b. $1.75
10($.10) + 3($.25)

c. $20d, 6q$

$\frac{3}{2}d + \frac{1}{3}q = d + q + 6$

$\frac{3}{2}d(10) + \frac{1}{3}q(25) = 10d + 25q$

d. $3.50. 20($.10) + 6($.25)

e. $\frac{10x}{3}$ dimes, x quarters

$\frac{3}{2}d + \frac{1}{3}q = d + q + x$

$\frac{3}{2}d(10) + \frac{1}{3}q(25) = 10d + 25q$

f. $\frac{\$1.75x}{3}$

$\frac{10x}{3}($.10) + x($.25)$

g. Since Theresa has $\frac{10x}{3}$ dimes, and since this must be a whole number, x has to be divisible by 3.

MIXTURES

Encourage your students to use hand calculators as an aid to solving the problems and in particular as an aid to checking the problems. (Checking a solution by taking 25% of $17\frac{87}{95}$ can be a rather messy undertaking even with a calculator, but at least the calculator will help the student decide whether or not a solution does check out without having the student worry about whether or not the multiplication and division involved was accurate.)

Along this same line, all answers given are exact unless the problem specifies that the answer is to be rounded. If an answer is $\dfrac{1702}{95}$, then the answer is $17\frac{87}{95}$, not 17.92 or 17.9158 or some other decimal approximation the student can get by using a hand calculator to divide 1702 by 95.

Insist that your students check their solutions. And when an approximated answer is called for, insist they check by using the exact answers rather than the approximated answers. As indicated above, checking some of the problems is tedious at best. But it pays off by teaching the student how to ascertain whether or not a given answer is correct without having to rely on an answer book, so that when the student tries to apply algebra in everyday life (s)he is much more likely to do so successfully than if (s)he had been trained merely to write equations and solve them and then check on their correctness by looking at an answer book.

Many students find it confusing to work with equations that contain decimals. Such students should be encouraged to eliminate decimals early in order to make their work easier. For example, if

$.90(1) = .45(1 + x),$

multiplying both sides by 100 gives

$90(1) = 45(1 + x),$

which is, for most students, a simpler equation to solve.

For problems about chemical mixtures, it may help the students do the problems more easily if you state the obvious:

Keep your percents consistent.

Example:

Problem: How much water should be added to one liter of a 90% alcohol solution to make it a 75% solution?

Discussion: Decide whether to set up the equation in terms of alcohol or in terms of water.

(1) If in terms of alcohol, then you have 90% of one liter, and you're going to add 0% of alcohol, and you're going to end up with 75% of alcohol. Put w = the amount of water to be added. Then $.90(1) + 0(w) = .75(1 + w)$, or $.90 = .75(1 + w)$.

(2) If in terms of water, then you have 10% of 1 liter, and you're going to add 100% of water, and you're going to end up with 25% of water. So $.10(1) + 1.00(w) = .25(1 + w)$, or $.10 + w = .25(1 + w)$.

(Note: It doesn't matter whether the 10% is water or something else in the 90% solution. We can talk in terms of "nonalcohol" instead of "water" and use n instead of w for the variable.)

Notice that either way of solving the problem—i.e., by (1) or by (2)—says $\dfrac{1}{5}$ liter of water is to be added.

Problems about mixing candy (or whatever) are analogous to coin problems, except that more money is involved. Notice that the systems of equations needed for solving these two problems are mathematically identical:

(1) Meecham has 14 nickels and dimes that total $1.00. How many of each are there?

$$n + d = 14$$
$$5n + 10d = 100 \text{ or } n + 2d = 20$$

(2) Meecham wants to mix 14 pounds of nougats and dates to sell for $50. If nougats are $2.50 a pound, and dates are $5 a pound, how many pounds of each should be used?

$$n + d = 14$$
$$2.50n + 5d = 50 \text{ or } n + 2d = 20$$

Students who have mastered coin problems but have trouble with such mixture problems can benefit from having the analogy made clear to them.

MIXTURES DETAILED SOLUTIONS

1. 1 liter
$$.90(1) = .45(1 + x)$$

2. 1 liter
$$.75(4) = .60(4 + x)$$

3. $\frac{1}{4}$ liter
$$.75(1) = .60(1 + x)$$

4. $\frac{3}{5}$ liter
$$.60(1) + 1.00(x) = .75(1 + x)$$

5. 125
$$.90(1000) = .80(1000 + x)$$

6. 300
$$.80(300) + 1.00(x) = .90(300 + x)$$

7. 5
$$3.00(5) + 4.00(x) = 3.50(5 + x)$$

8. a. 9 liters. $0(1) + 1.00w = .90(1 + w)$

   b. $\frac{1}{9}$ liters. $0(1) + 1.00h = .10(1 + h)$

9. a. 38 liters
$$0(2) + 1.00(i) = .95(2 + i)$$

   b. $\frac{2}{19}$ liter
$$0(2) + 1.00(a) = .05(2 + a)$$

10. $\frac{1}{4}$ liter. $1.00(1) + 0(w) = .80(1 + w)$

11. $\frac{1}{7}$ liter. $.80(1) + 0(w) = .70(1 + w)$

12. a. 8. $2.00j + 2.75(4) = 2.25(j + 4)$

   b. 2. $2.00j + 2.75(4) = 2.50(j + 4)$

13. a. $\frac{2}{5}$ liter
$$.70(2) + 1.00(a) = .75(2 + a)$$

   b. 1 liter
$$.70(2) + 1.00(a) = .80(2 + a)$$

   c. 4 liters
$$.70(2) + 1.00(a) = .90(2 + a)$$

   d. $\frac{2}{13}$ liter
$$.70(2) + 0w = .65(2 + w)$$

   e. $\frac{1}{3}$ liter
$$.70(2) + 0w = .60(2 + w)$$

   f. $\frac{4}{5}$ liter
$$.70(2) + 0w = .50(2 + w)$$

14. a. $3\frac{9}{37}$ pounds, OR just under $3\frac{1}{4}$ pounds.
$$.10(15) + 1.00x = .26(15 + x)$$

b. $1\frac{7}{8}$ pounds, OR 1 pound 14 ounces
$.10(15) + 1.00x = .20(15 + x)$

15. a. 1 pint
$.50(1) + 1.00m = .75(1 + m)$

b. 2 pints
$1 + 1$

c. $\frac{1}{3}$ pint
$.50(1) - 1.00c = .25(1 - c)$

d. $\frac{2}{3}$ pint
$1 - \frac{1}{3}$

e. $\frac{1}{3}$ pint
$.50(1) - 1.00m = .25(1 - m)$

f. $\frac{2}{3}$ pint
$1 - \frac{1}{3}$

g. 1 pint
$.50(1) + 1.00c = .75(1 + c)$

h. 2 pints
$1 + 1$

16. a. 2 liters
$.90(2) + 1.00w = .95(2 + w)$

b. 4 liters
$2 + 2$

c. $\frac{2}{17}$ liter
$.10(2) + 1.00a = .15(2 + a)$

d. $2\frac{2}{17}$ liters
$2 + \frac{2}{17}$

17. a. 5 pounds of each.
$c + e = 10$
$2.50c + 3.50e = 3.00(10)$

b. $7\frac{1}{2}$ pounds @ $2.50; $2\frac{1}{2}$ pounds at $3.50
$c + e = 10$
$2.50c + 3.50e = 2.75(10)$

c. $2\frac{1}{2}$ pounds @ 2.50; $7\frac{1}{2}$ pounds at $3.50
$c + e = 10$
$2.50c + 3.50e = 3.25(10)$

18. a. $2\frac{2}{3}$ grams
$8 - A = .25(24 - A)$

b. $6\frac{2}{9}$ grams
$8 - A = .10(24 - A)$

c. $13\frac{1}{3}$ grams
$16 - B = .25(24 - B)$

d. $15\frac{1}{9}$ grams
$16 - B = .10(24 - B)$

19. $7\frac{1}{2}$ of each
$4.25(15) = 5.50e + 3.00c$
$e + c = 15$

20. 6 of the cheaper, 4 of the more expensive
$3.50(10) = 2.50c + 5.00e$
$c + e = 10$

21. a. 16 pounds of Brazilian, 4 pounds of Columbian
$B + C = 20$
$4B + 9C = 5(20)$

b. 10 pounds of Brazilian, 10 pounds of Columbian
$B + C = 20$
$4B + 9C = 6.50(20)$

c. 4 pounds of Brazilian, 16 pounds of Columbian
$B + C = 20$
$4B + 9C = 8(20)$

22. a. 30. $.70C + .90(10) = .75(C + 10)$

b. 10. $.70C + .90(10) = .80(C + 10)$

c. $3\frac{1}{3}$ $.70C + .90(10) = .85(C + 10)$

d. $6\frac{2}{3}$ $.70C + .90(10) = .82(C + 10)$

e. $\dfrac{900 - 10p}{p - 70}$

$.70C + .90(10) = \dfrac{p}{100}(C + 10)$

23. a. 5. $2p + 5(10) = 4(p + 10)$

b. 20. $2p + 5(10) = 3(p + 10)$

c. $3\frac{1}{3}$ pounds of peanuts; $6\frac{2}{3}$ pound of mixed nuts.
$p + m = 10$ $2p + 5m = 4(10)$

d. $6\frac{2}{3}$ pound of peanuts, $3\frac{1}{3}$ pounds of mixed nuts
$p + m = 10$
$2p + 5m = 3(10)$

24. a. 7500 pounds of 5% lead, 2500 pounds of 17% lead
$f + s = 10,000$
$.05f + .17s = .08(10,000)$

b. 3750 pounds of 5% lead, 6250 pounds of 27% lead
$f + s = 10,000$
$.05f + .17s = .125(10,000)$

25. a. $3\frac{1}{3}$ pounds of Merion, $6\frac{2}{3}$ pounds of Kentucky
$M + K = 10$
$8.00M + 6.50K = 7.00(10)$

b. $7\frac{1}{2}$ pounds of each
$M + K = 15$
$8.00M + 6.50K = 7.25(15)$

c. $5\frac{1}{3}$ pounds of Merion, $2\frac{2}{3}$ pounds

of Kentucky
$M + K = 8$
$8.00M + 6.50K = 7.50(8)$

26. a. 3 pounds $5\frac{1}{3}$ ounces of Merion,
6 pounds $10\frac{2}{3}$ ounces of Kentucky
ounces = $\frac{1}{3}$ of 16 and $\frac{2}{3}$ of 16

b. 7 pounds 8 ounces of each
ounces = $\frac{1}{2}$ of 16 for each

c. 5 pounds $5\frac{1}{3}$ ounces of Merion,
2 pounds $10\frac{2}{3}$ ounces of Kentucky
ounces = $\frac{1}{3}$ of 16 and $\frac{2}{3}$ of 16

27. a. $7\frac{1}{2}$ pounds of bologna, $2\frac{1}{2}$ pounds of salami
$b + s = 10$
$1.50b + 2.50s = 1.75(10)$

b. 5 pounds of each
$b + s = 10$
$1.50b + 2.50s = 2.00(10)$

c. $2\frac{1}{2}$ pounds of bologna, $7\frac{1}{2}$ pounds of salami
$b + s = 10$
$1.50b + 2.50s = 2.25(10)$

28. a. 4 loads of coars, 6 loads of fine
$c + f = 10$
$40c + 60f = 52(10)$

b. 12 loads of coarse, 3 loads of fine
$c + f = 15$
$40c + 60f = 44(15)$

29. Regular marbles are 2¢ each; shooters are 8¢ each. Put a = the average selling price—i.e., for part a, $a = 3$¢; for part b, $a = 4$¢; and so on. Then the equations are
$r + s = 100$
$2r + 8s = a(100)$.

a. 83 regular, 17 shooter
b. 67 regular, 33 shooter
c. 50 of each
d. 33 regular, 67 shooter
e. 17 regular, 83 shooter
f. 0 regular, 100 shooter

30. a. $2\frac{1}{2}$ dozen, or 30, of each kind
$c + e = 5$
$2.00c + 2.50e = 5(2.25)$

b. 8 dozen @ $2, 2 dozen @ $2.50
$c + e = 10$
$2.00c + 2.50e = 10(2.10)$

c. 1 dozen @ $2, 4 dozen @ $2.50
$c + e = 5$
$2.00c + 2.50e = 2.40(5)$

31. If c = the number of carats desired—i.e., 12 for part a, 15 for part b, 16 for part c, then the equations are

$$t + e = 90$$

$$\frac{10}{24}t + \frac{18}{24}e = \frac{c}{24}(90).$$

a. $67\frac{1}{2}$ ounces of 10-carat gold,
$22\frac{1}{2}$ ounces of 18-carat gold.

b. $33\frac{3}{4}$ ounce of 10-carat gold, $56\frac{1}{4}$ ounces of 18-carat gold

c. $22\frac{1}{2}$ ounces of 10-carat gold,
$67\frac{1}{2}$ ounces of 18-carat gold

32. a. $1\frac{1}{19}$ yards
$1.00(20) + 0s = .95(20 + s)$ OR
$0(20) + 1.00s = .05(20 + s)$

b. 380 yards
$1.00(20) + 0t = .05(20 + t)$ OR
$0(20) + 1.00(t) = .95(20 + t)$

33. a. $7\frac{1}{2}$
$4.25(15) = 3.50c + 5.00e$
$c + e = 15$

b. $5.00 a pound. (Why?)
The price of the mixture is to increase, so the candy used must sell for more than the mixture does.

c. $7\frac{1}{2}$ pounds
$4.25(15) + 5.00e = 4.50(15 + e)$

d. $22\frac{1}{2}$
$15 + 7\frac{1}{2}$

e. $3.50 a pound
The price of the mixture is to decrease, so the candy used must sell for less than the mixture does.

f. 30 pounds
$4.25(15) + 3.50c = 3.75(15 + c)$

g. 45
$15 + 30$

34. a. $6\frac{2}{3}$ liters of 70% solution,
$3\frac{1}{3}$ liters of 85% solution
$s + e = 10$
$.70s + .85e = .75(10)$

b. $3\frac{1}{3}$ liters of 70% solution,
$6\frac{2}{3}$ liters of 85% solution
$s + e = 10$
$.70s + .85e = .80(10)$

35. a. 6 pounds @ $3.50,
4 pounds @ $4.75
$c + e = 10$
$3.50c + 4.75e = 4.00(10)$

b. 3.2 pounds @ $3.50,
4.8 pounds @ $4.75

$c + e = 8$

$3.50c + 4.75e = 4.25(8)$

Answers using fractions are $3\frac{1}{5}$ and $4\frac{4}{5}$.

c. 9.6 pounds @ $3.50,

2.4 pounds @ 44.75

$c + e = 12$

$3.50c + 4.75e = 3.75(12)$

Answers using fractions are $9\frac{3}{5}$ and $2\frac{2}{5}$.

36. a. not applicable

b. 3 pounds 3.2 ounces @ $3.50,
4 pounds 12.8 ounces @ $4.75

ounces = .2 of 16 and .8 of 16. If fractions are preferred, then

ounces = $\frac{1}{5}$ of 16 and $\frac{4}{5}$ of 16,

or $3\frac{1}{5}$ and $12\frac{4}{5}$.

c. 9 pounds 9.6 ounces @ $3.50,
2 pounds 6.4 ounces @ $4.75

ounces = .6 of 16 and .4 of 16. In

fractions, that's $\frac{3}{5}$ of 16 and $\frac{2}{5}$

of 16, or $9\frac{3}{5}$ and $6\frac{2}{5}$.

37. 10. $2.25(15) + 3.00x = 2.55(15 + x)$

OR $\dfrac{2.25(15) + 3.00x}{15 + x} = 2.55$

38. a. $6\frac{2}{3}$. $.60(10 + x) = 1.00(10)$

b. $2\frac{1}{2}$. $.80(10 + x) = 1.00(10)$

c. 30. $.25(10 + x) = 1.00(10)$ OR
$.75(10 + x) = 1.00x$

d. 70. $.80(30) = 1.00(10) + \dfrac{x}{100}(20)$

e. 12. Notice that he has to buy two more pounds of sunflower

seeds before he can have such a mixture.

$.60(20) + 1.00x = .75(20 + x)$

39. a. $\dfrac{1}{95}$ quart

$.04(1) + 1.00(c) = .05(1 + c)$

b. $1\frac{1}{95}$ quart. $1 + \dfrac{1}{95}$

c. $\dfrac{1}{5}$ quart

$.96(1) - 1.00(m) = .95(1 - m)$

d. $\dfrac{4}{5}$ quart. $1 - \dfrac{1}{5}$

e. $\dfrac{1}{3}$ quart

$.96(1) + 1.00(m) = .97(1 + m)$

f. $1\frac{1}{3}$ quart. $1 + \dfrac{1}{3}$

g. $\dfrac{1}{97}$ quart

$.04(1) - 1.00(c) = .03(1 - c)$

h. $\dfrac{96}{97}$ quart. $1 - \dfrac{1}{97}$

40. The numerical answers don't change at all. Only the units change.
a. "Quart" becomes "liter."
b. "Quart" becomes "gallon."
c. "Quart" becomes "half-gallon."

41. a. 9. $\dfrac{x}{100}(25) + 1.00(10) = .35(35)$

b. $12\frac{1}{2}$ pounds

$.10(25) + 1.00(x) = .40(25 + x)$

c. 75. $.80x + 0(25) = .60(x + 25)$

42. a. A is 10%; B is $17\frac{1}{2}$%; C is 10%

$$.30(\tfrac{1}{3}) + 0(\tfrac{2}{3}) = \tfrac{A}{100} \ (1)$$

$$.70(\tfrac{1}{4}) + 0(\tfrac{3}{4}) = \tfrac{B}{100} \ (1)$$

$$.60(\tfrac{1}{6}) + 0(\tfrac{5}{6}) = \tfrac{C}{100} \ (1)$$

b. 50%

$$.30(\tfrac{1}{3}) + .70(\tfrac{1}{4}) + .60(\tfrac{1}{6}) =$$

$$\tfrac{p}{100}(\tfrac{1}{3} + \tfrac{1}{4} + \tfrac{1}{6})$$

c. $37\frac{1}{2}$%

$$\tfrac{1}{3} + \tfrac{1}{4} + \tfrac{1}{6} = \tfrac{3}{4}; \text{ then use}$$

answer b for the easy way:

$$.50(\tfrac{3}{4}) + 0(\tfrac{1}{4}) = \tfrac{p}{100} \ (1)$$

d. $12\frac{1}{2}$%

Start with answer c and figure

that each bottle will start out $\frac{1}{3}$

full of $37\frac{1}{2}$% alcohol solution.

Then $.375(\tfrac{1}{3}) + 0(\tfrac{2}{3}) = \tfrac{p}{100} \ (1)$

43. a 96 ounces of orange juice
32 ounces of grapefruit juice

b. 64 ounces of each

c. 32 ounces of orange juice,
96 ounces of grapefruit juice
It may be easier to solve the
problem if we think of an 8-
ounce glass of juice as one unit.

Then 128 ounces is $\frac{128 \text{ ounces}}{8 \text{ ounces}} =$

16, and we have the system of
equations

$$j + g = 16$$
$$1.50j + 2.50g = s(16),$$

where $s = 1.75$ in part a, 2.00 in
part b, and 2.25 in part c. The
solutions for j and g will be
multiplied by 8 to get the
desired results.
We could, of course, obtain the
answers directly by using this
system:

$$j + g = 128 \ 1.50(\tfrac{j}{8})$$

$$= 2.50(\tfrac{g}{8}) = s(\tfrac{128}{8}),$$

but the students may find the
reasoning harder to follow here
than in the first system shown
above.

44. a. $4 a pound

$$2.00(\tfrac{1}{2}) + x(1 - \tfrac{1}{2}) = 3.00(1)$$

b. $3.45 a pound (Exact answer is
11 pounds for $38.)

$$2.00(\tfrac{5}{16}) + x(1 - \tfrac{5}{16}) = 3.00(1) \text{ or}$$
$$2.00(5) + x(16 - 5) = 3.00(16)$$

Note that the exact answer is
$3\frac{5}{11}$ a pound, which is
approximately $3.45 a pound.

c. $4.67 a pound (Exact answer is 3
pounds for $14.)

$$2.00(\tfrac{10}{16}) + x(1 - \tfrac{10}{16}) = 3.00(1) \text{ or}$$
$$2.00(10) + x(16 - 10) = 3.00(16)$$

The exact answer is $4\frac{2}{3}$, which
is approximately $4.67.

45. a. 50 pounds of round, 30 pounds of chuck, 20 pounds of suet
$r + c + s = 100$
$2.00r + 1.50c + .25s = 1.50(100)$
$s = .20(100)$

b. $2\frac{1}{2}$ pounds of round, $72\frac{1}{2}$ pounds of chuck, 25 pounds of suet
$r + c + s = 100$
$2.00r + 1.50c + .25s = 1.20(100)$
$s = .25(100)$

c. 60 pounds of round, 40 pounds of chuck
$r + c = 100$
$2.00r + 1.50c = 1.80(100)$

d. $1.56\frac{1}{4}$ a pound OR
4 pounds for $6.25
$s = .25(100)$
$s + r = 100$
$.25s + 2.00r = x(100)$
(Solve for x.)

e. $1.18\frac{3}{4}$ a pound OR
4 pounds for $4.75
$s = .25(100)$
$s + c = 100$
$.25s + 1.50c = x(100)$
(Solve for x.)

f. $1.37\frac{1}{2}$ a pound OR
2 pounds for $2.75
$s = .25(100)$
$r = c$ $r + c + s = 100$
$2.00r + 1.50c + .25s = x(100)$
(Solve for x.)

46. There are 16(3), or 48, ounces in 3 pounds of meat, so the chuck steak is $\frac{5}{48}$ suet, and the round steak is $\frac{3}{48}$ suet.

a. $30\frac{5}{19}$ pounds of round, $57\frac{12}{19}$ pounds of chuck, $12\frac{2}{19}$ pounds of suet
$r + c + s = 100$ OR
$(\frac{45}{48}r + \frac{43}{48}c) + (\frac{3}{48}r + \frac{5}{48}c + s) = 100$
$\frac{3}{48}r + \frac{5}{48}c + 1.00s = .20(100)$
$2.00r + 1.50c + .25s = 1.50(100)$

b. Not possible, since equations work out to $-21\frac{16}{19}$ pounds of round, $106\frac{11}{19}$ pounds of chuck, $15\frac{5}{19}$ pounds of suet $r + c + s = 100$ OR (See part **a** above.)
$\frac{3}{48}r + \frac{5}{48}c + 1.00s = .25(100)$
$2.00r + 1.50c + .25s + 1.20(100)$

c. $29\frac{7}{37}$ pounds of round, $81\frac{3}{37}$ pound of chuck
$\frac{45}{48}r + \frac{43}{48}c = 100$
$2.00r + 1.50c + 1.80(100)$

Notice that the answer, $29\frac{7}{37}$ pounds of round and $81\frac{3}{37}$ pounds of chuck, totals $110\frac{10}{37}$ pounds of meat, implying that a total of $10\frac{10}{37}$ pounds of suet had to be trimmed from the two kinds of steak. We can check this by taking $\frac{3}{48}(29\frac{7}{37}) + \frac{5}{48}(81\frac{3}{37})$, since $\frac{3}{48}$ of the round steak is suet and $\frac{5}{48}$ of the chuck steak

is suet.

d. $1.65 a pound

$\frac{3}{48} r + s = .25(100)$

$r + s = 100$
$2.00r + .25s = x(100)$
(This works out to 80 pounds of
round, 20 pounds of suet. Solve for x to
get the required answer.)

e. $1.30 a pound (Exact answer is

$1\frac{51}{172}$ a pound, OR

$223 for 172 pounds, OR

$55.75 for 43 pounds.)

$\frac{5}{48} c + s = .25(100)$

$c + s = 100$
$1.50c + .25s = x(100)$
(This works out to $83\frac{31}{43}$ pounds of
chuck, $16\frac{12}{43}$ pounds of suet. Solve for x to
get the required answer.)

f. $1.48 a pound. (Exact answer is

$1\frac{21}{44}$ a pound OR $65 for 44

pounds, OR $16.25 for 11
pounds.)

$\frac{5}{48} c + \frac{3}{48} r + s = .25(100)$

$r = c$
$c + r + s = 100$
$1.50c + 2.00r + .25s = x(100)$
(This works out to $40\frac{10}{11}$ pounds each
of round and chuck, $18\frac{2}{11}$ pounds of suet.
Solve for x to get the required answer.)

47. 15,625. $.98(.96p) + 2(.02)(.96p) =$
15,300

48. $60 of A, $40 of B
$.20A + .25B = .22(100)$
$A + B = 100$

49. $59.02 of A, $40.98 of B (Answers
before rounding to the nearest cent

are: $59\frac{1}{61}$ of A, $40\frac{60}{61}$ of B.)

This is a good opportunity to point
out to the students that if some
percentage is added to the cost of
merchandise (in order to obtain a
selling price), then that same
percentage deducted from the
selling price will not give the cost.
For example, if 25% is added to a
cost of $80, then that is $20 to be
added, giving a selling price of $100.
But if 25% of $100, which is $25, is
deducted from $100, the result is
$75, not $80. Given a selling price,
say $100, and the percent of cost
added to the merchandise sold, say
25%, we arrive at the cost by
reasoning as follows. The
merchandise was sold for its cost
(c) plus 25% of its cost ($.25c$), or a
total of $1.25c$. Thus, $1.25c = 100$, and
$c = \frac{100}{1.25}$.

Letting A and B be the selling prices
of the merchandise in the given
problem, then we get the following
system of equations.

$$A + B = 100$$

$$\frac{A}{1.20} + \frac{B}{1.25} = \frac{100}{1.22}$$

50. a. 12 ounces of zinnia seeds,
4 ounces of margold seeds
$z + m = 16(1)$
$6z + 8m = 6.50(16)(1)$

b. 8 ounces of zinnia seeds,
24 ounces of marigold seeds

$z + m = 16(2)$
$6z + 8m = 7.50(16)(2)$

c. 30 ounces of zinnia seeds,
50 ounces of marigold seeds
$z + m = 16(5)$
$6z + 8m = 7.25(16)(5)$

d. $8p(8 - s)$ ounces of zinnia seeds
$8p(s - 6)$ ounces of marigold seeds
$z + m = 16(p)$
$6z + 8m = s(16)(p)$

51. a. $\dfrac{16p(M - s)}{M - Z}$ ounces of zinnia seeds,

$\dfrac{16p(s - Z)}{M - Z}$ ounces of marigold

seeds.
$z + m = 16p$
$Zz + Mm = s(16p)$
(Solve for z and m.)

b. $M = Z$
If $M = Z$, then $M - Z = 0$, and we
can't divide by zero.

c. $s = M = Z$
Substitute Z for M in the second
equation and get

$Z(z + m) = 16ps.$

Now substitute in this equation
from the first equation and get

$Z(16p) = 16ps.$

Divide both sides by $16p$ and get

$Z = s.$

52. Note: The equations here use the
answers from problem 50.

a. $91\frac{1}{4}$

$.90(12) + .95(4) = \dfrac{p}{100}(16)$

b. $93\frac{3}{4}$

$.90(8) + .95(24) = \dfrac{p}{100}(16)(2)$ OR

$.90(\frac{1}{2}) + .95(1\frac{1}{2}) = \dfrac{p}{100}(2)$

c. $93\frac{1}{8}$

$.90(30) + .95(50) = \dfrac{p}{100}(16)(5)$

OR $.90(1\frac{7}{8}) + .95(3\frac{1}{8}) = \dfrac{p}{100}(5)$

d. $1\frac{1}{9}$ pounds. $.90w = 1$

e. $1\frac{1}{19}$ pounds. $.95w = 1$

f-h. Note: Use the answers to
problem 50 and to problem 52d-e.

f. $13\frac{1}{3}$ ounces of zinnia seeds,

$4\frac{4}{19}$ ounces of marigold seeds

zinnia, $12(1\frac{1}{9})$; marigold, $4(1\frac{1}{19})$

g. $8\frac{8}{9}$ ounces of zinnia seeds,

$25\frac{5}{19}$ ounces of marigold seeds

zinnia, $8(1\frac{1}{9})$; marigold, $24(1\frac{1}{19})$

h. $33\frac{1}{3}$ ounces of zinnia seeds,

$52\frac{12}{19}$ ounces of marigold seeds

zinnia, $30(1\frac{1}{9})$; marigold, $50(1\frac{1}{19})$

i-k. Note: The problems become
simpler if the given prices are
adjusted to reflect the extra
weight given because of the lack
of germination. That is, suppose
the price is \$10 an ounce for a
seed with a 90% germination
rate. Since the customer is
charged only for the seeds that
germinate, we can either figure
an actual price of \$9 an ounce
(that is, 90% of \$10 an ounce),

or we can figure an actual weight of $1\frac{1}{9}$ ounces for the $10 price (that is, 90%$w$ = 1 ounce, so w = $1\frac{1}{9}$ ounces). In the solutions below, selling prices per ounce are figured as:

zinnias, 90% of $6, or $5.40; marigolds, 95% of $8, or $7.60.

i. 8 ounces of each kind
$z + m = 16(1)$
$5.40z + 7.60m = 6.50(16)(1)$

j. $1\frac{5}{11}$ ounces of zinnia seeds,

$30\frac{6}{11}$ ounces of marigold seeds
$z + m = (16)(2)$
$5.40z + 7.60m = 7.50(16)(2)$

k. $12\frac{8}{11}$ ounces of zinnia seeds,

$67\frac{3}{11}$ ounces of marigold seeds
$z + m = (16)(5)$
$5.40z + 7.60m = 7.25(16)(5)$

53. a. 14 ounces
$0(128) + 1.00c = .10(128 + c)$

b. 142 ounces
$128 + 14$

c. 43 ounces
$0(128) + 1.00t = .25(128 + t)$

d. 171 ounces
$128 + 43$

e-f. Since only the carrot and tomato juices have been included, the original 128 ounces is not 10% carrot juice and 25% tomato juice. But the owner intended to have the usual mixture, so we must assume he prepared the two juices in the ratio of 10:25.

Consequently, we assume the original mixture is $\frac{10}{35}$ carrot juice, $\frac{25}{35}$ tomato juice.

e. 238 ounces
$0(128) + 1.00j = .65(128 + j)$

f. 366 ounces
$128 + 238$

54. a. 5 ounces   **b.** 142 ounces
c. 148 ounces

a–c. 25% of the 128-ounce mixture, or 32 ounces, is tomato juice. Then 128 – 32, or 96, ounces is "other" juices, and these must total 65% of the corrected mixture. So we start by solving the equation $.65t = 96$, and find that the total mixture

must be $\frac{9600}{65}$ ounces, or $147\frac{9}{13}$

ounces. Carrot juice must be 10%

of this, so we have $14\frac{10}{13}$ ounces

of carrot juice. Tomato juice

must be 25% of $147\frac{9}{13}$, so we will

have a total of $36\frac{12}{13}$ ounces of tomato juice, of which the mixture already contains 32

ounces, leaving $4\frac{12}{13}$ ounces to be

added.

d–f. d. 5 ounces   **e.** 44 ounces
f. 177 ounces
See the discussion of a–c above. 10% of 128 = 12.8, leaving 115.2 of "other" juices. Then

$.65t = 115.2$, and $t = \frac{11520}{65}$, or

$177\frac{3}{13}$. The tomato juice to be

added is 25% of $177\frac{3}{13}$ ounces =

$44\frac{4}{13}$ ounces. The carrot juice to be added is 10% of $177\frac{3}{13}$ ounces = $17\frac{47}{65}$ ounces, minus $12\frac{4}{5}$ ounces of carrot juice already there, leaving $4\frac{12}{13}$ ounces of carrot juice to be added.

55. Here is a step-by-step proof:
- a) Put m = the number of units (ounces, gallons, liters, whatever) in the erroneous mixture.
- b) Put t = the number of units in the corrected mixture.
- c) Put C = the percentage (expressed as a decimal) of carrot juice supposed to be included.
- d) Put T = the percentage (expressed as a decimal) of tomato juice supposed to be included.
- e) From c and d, $1 - (C + T)$ = the percentage (expressed as a decimal) of "other" juices supposed to be included.
- f) From c and a, Cm = the number of units of carrot juice in the erroneous mixture when the tomato juice had been omitted.
- g) From d and a, Tm = the number of units of tomato juice in the erroneous mixture when the carrot juice had been omitted.
- h) From a and f, $m - Cm = m(1 - C)$ = the number of units of "other" juices when the tomato juice had been omitted.
- i) From a and g, $m - Tm = m(1 - T)$ = the number of units of "other" juices when the carrot juice had been omitted.
- j) From e and b and h, $[1 - (C + T)]t$

= $m(1 - C)$, so $t = \dfrac{m(1 - C)}{1 - (C + T)}$ when the tomato juice had been omitted.

- k) From e and b and i, $[1 - (C + T)]t$

= $m(1 - T)$, so $t = \dfrac{m(1 - T)}{1 - (C + T)}$ when the carrot juice had been omitted.

- l) From j and c, $\dfrac{Cm(1 - C)}{1 - (C + T)}$ = the number of units of carrot juice to be included in the corrected mixture when the tomato juice had been omitted.

- m) From k and d, $\dfrac{Tm(1 - T)}{1 - (C + T)}$ = the number of units of tomato juice to be included in the corrected mixture when the carrot juice had been omitted.

- n) From l and f, $\dfrac{Cm(1 - C)}{1 - (C + T)} - Cm$ = the number of units of carrot juice to be added when the tomato juice had been omitted.

- o) From m and g, $\dfrac{Tm(1 - T)}{1 - (C + T)} - Tm$ = the number of units of tomato juice to be added when the carrot juice had been omitted.

So, using n and o, the question is

$$\frac{Cm(1 - C)}{1 - (C + T)} - Cm \stackrel{?}{=} \frac{Tm(1 - T)}{1 - (C + T)} - Tm$$

Now we manipulate each side of the (questionable) equation:

$$\frac{Cm(1-C)-Cm[1-(C+T)]}{1-(C+T)} \overset{?}{=} \frac{Tm(1-T)-Tm[1-(C+T)]}{1-(C+T)}$$

$$\frac{Cm-C^2m-Cm+C^2m+CTm}{1-(C+T)} \overset{?}{=} \frac{Tm-T^2m-Tm+TCm=T^2m}{1-(C+T)}$$

$$\frac{CTm}{1-(C+T)} = \frac{CTm}{1-(C+T)}$$

Thus we have proved that the amount of carrot juice to be added when the tomato juice had been omitted is always the same as the amount of tomato juice to be added when the carrot juice had been omitted. This assumes, of course, that $1-(C+T) \neq 0$, or, in other words, that there are, in fact, juices other than carrot juice and tomato juice that the mixture is supposed to include.

FORMULAS, RECTANGLES, D = rt

For problems involving rectangles, encourage the students to draw and label diagrams, particularly when there are borders involved. It's nice to be able to do everything mentally, but it's much easier to have a picture of the problem staring one in the face.

For distance, rate, and time problems, you may have to keep reminding the students that $D = rt$ and the formula is meant to be used. Stress to them that all three variables are to be in compatible units. For example, if r is in miles per hour, then t has to be in hours and D has to be in miles. If D is in kilometers and t is in minutes, then r has to be in kilometers per minute.

Although I generally detest the use of the term "cancel" in mathematics (because the students tend to cancel the most ineligible items in an expression), it is a useful concept when trying to convert

from one unit of measurement to another. For this purpose, the word "per" can be interpreted as "divided by."

Example:

Suppose we know a rate is r miles per hour and we want to convert it to feet per second. We have $\frac{(r)(miles)}{hours}$. There are $\frac{(5,280)(feet)}{miles}$ and $\frac{(3,600)(seconds)}{hours}$. In order to get the terms into the positions we want, we write

$$\frac{(r)(miles)(5,280)(feet)(hours)}{(hours)(miles)(3,600)(seconds)}$$

Now we can cancel(!) the two "miles" and the two "hours" and find that r miles per hour = $\frac{5280}{3600} r$ feet per second.

The distance formula is an everyday example of inverse variation. It is a common error, however, to regard it as a direct variation. A good example of this is the usual reaction to the question, "If a car averaged 40 mph from A to B and 50 mph on the return trip, what was the overall average for the round trip?" The usual answer is 45 mph. The correct answer is $44\frac{4}{9}$ mph.

Although an attempt was made to place the problems (within a section) in increasing order of difficulty, it was hard to decide whether a problem involving a general quadratic equation should automatically be placed after a problem involving only linear equations and a problem requiring only the taking of a square root. I finally decided against it, and the result is that the difficulty level is judged according to the answers to these questions: (1) How hard will the student find it to set up the initial equations? (2) Once the equations are set up, how hard will the student find it to figure out what to do with them? (3) Once the student figures out what to do with them, (a) how hard will the manipulations be? (b) will an intermediate answer have to be found and then used to find the final answer? (c) is the problem complex enough so that the student might lose himself or herself in the middle and have to reconstruct his or her strategy?

With those questions in mind, it seems to me that problem A below is a much simpler problem to solve than problem B, even though A involves solving an equation of the form $ax^2 + bx + c = 0$ and B does not.

A: A rectangle is 5 cm longer than it is wide. Its area is 66 sq cm. What are its dimensions?

B: A rectangle whose width is two-thirds of its length is surrounded by an outside border two feet wide. If the area of the rectangle is 1350 sq ft, what is the area of the border?

Consequently, if your class has not yet learned to solve general quadratic equations, you will have to be careful to skip assigning problems that require such knowledge.

Encourage the use of hand calculators for the last two sections (RECTANGLES and D = rt). Not only are some solutions tedious otherwise, but the student is likely to get bogged down in arithmetic and lose track of where s(he) is in the problem and what that particular computation was supposed to accomplish.

FORMULAS, RECTANGLES, AND D=rt
DETAILED SOLUTIONS

1. a. $A = lw$

b. $P = 2l + 2w$;   **c.** $P = 2(l + w)$

d. $C = \pi d$;   **e.** $A = \pi r^2$

f. $A = \dfrac{1}{2}ba$ **g.** $A = d(1 + r)^n$

2. a. $A + 15 = (b + 6)(c - 2)$

b. $2A = (b + 6)(c + 2)$

c. A is doubled.   **d.** A is unchanged.

e. A is six times as much.

f. A is doubled.

g. A is $2\frac{1}{4}$ times as much.

h. b is halved.

i. b is $\dfrac{2}{9}$ as much.

3. a. $A + 40 = (l + 5)w$

b. $A = \dfrac{2}{3}\, l^2$;   **c.** $2A = (l + 5)(w + 2)$

d. $A + 10 = l(w + \dfrac{1}{2})$;

e. $3A = (l + \dfrac{2}{3})(w + \dfrac{1}{4})$

f. No change. $2l\left(\dfrac{w}{2}\right) = lw = A$

g. A is six times as much.
$2l(3w) = 6lw = 6A$

h. A is $\dfrac{1}{6}$ as much.

$\dfrac{1}{4}l\left(\dfrac{2}{3}w\right) = \dfrac{1}{6}lw = \dfrac{1}{6}A$

i. A is $\frac{3}{4}$ as much.

$$\frac{1}{4}l\,(3w) = \frac{3}{4}lw = \frac{3}{4}A$$

j. A is $\frac{3}{4}$ as much.

$$3l\left(\frac{1}{4}w\right) = \frac{3}{4}lw = \frac{3}{4}A$$

k-p. $w = \frac{A}{l}$, so

k. w is doubled. $\frac{2A}{l} = 2\left(\frac{A}{l}\right) = 2w$

l. w is unchanged. $\frac{2A}{2l} = \frac{A}{l} = w$

m. w is $\frac{2}{3}$ as much.

$$\frac{2A}{3l} = \frac{2}{3}\left(\frac{A}{l}\right) = \frac{2}{3}w$$

n. w is $\frac{3}{8}$ as much.

$$\frac{\frac{3}{4}A}{2l} = \frac{3}{8}\left(\frac{A}{l}\right) = \frac{3}{8}w$$

o. w is $2\frac{2}{3}$ as much.

$$\frac{2A}{\frac{3}{4}l} = \frac{8}{3}\left(\frac{A}{l}\right) = \frac{8}{3}w$$

p. w is $\frac{8}{9}$ as much.

$$\frac{\frac{2}{3}A}{\frac{3}{4}l} = \frac{8}{9}\left(\frac{A}{l}\right) = \frac{8}{9}w$$

4. $C = 2\pi r$

5. a. A is four times as much.
$k(2r)^2 = 4(kr^2) = 4A$

b. A is $\frac{1}{9}$ as much.
$k\left(\frac{1}{3}r\right)^2 = \frac{1}{9}(kr^2) = \frac{1}{9}A$

c. $A + 30 = k(r + 2)^2$

d. $\frac{A}{2} = k(r - 3)^2$

6. a. $S + 15 = \dfrac{(n + 1)(n + 2)}{2}$

b. $S + n + 1 = \dfrac{(n + 1)(n + 2)}{2}$

c. $S - 345 = \dfrac{\frac{n}{2}\left(\frac{n}{2} + 1\right)}{2}$ OR

$S - 345 = \dfrac{n(n + 2)}{8}$

d. $S + 26 = \dfrac{2n(2n + 1)}{2}$ OR

$S + 26 = n(2n + 1)$

7. a. $D = (r + 10)\,(t - 1)$

b. $D = (r - 15)\,(t + 2)$

c. $D + 40 = (r + 8)\left(t - \dfrac{30}{60}\right)$

d. $2D + 50 = 2r\left(t + \dfrac{20}{60}\right)$

e. $D - 250 = (r + 10)\,(t - 10)$

f. D is four times as great.
$(2r)(2t) = 4(rt) = 4D$

g. D is unchanged.

$(2r)(\frac{t}{2}) = rt = D$

h. D is unchanged.

$\frac{r}{2}(2t) = rt = D$

i. D is half as much.

$(\frac{2}{3}r)(\frac{3}{4}t) = \frac{1}{2}(rt) = \frac{1}{2}D$

j. D is one-third as much.

$(\frac{4}{3}r)(\frac{1}{4}t) = \frac{1}{3}(rt) = \frac{1}{3}D$

k. D is $\frac{3}{8}$ as much.

$(\frac{3}{2}r)(\frac{1}{4}t) = \frac{3}{8}(rt) = \frac{3}{8}D$

l-o. $t = \frac{D}{r}$, so

l. t is doubled.

$\frac{D}{\frac{r}{2}} = 2(\frac{D}{r}) = 2t$

m. $t = \frac{D}{r}$, so t is four times as much.

$\frac{2D}{\frac{r}{2}} = 4(\frac{D}{r}) = 4t$

n. $t = \frac{D}{r}$, so t is $\frac{3}{4}$ as much.

$\frac{\frac{D}{2}}{\frac{2}{3}r} = \frac{3}{4}(\frac{D}{r}) = \frac{3}{4}t$

o. $t = \frac{D}{r}$, so t is $1\frac{1}{8}$ times as much.

$\frac{\frac{3}{4}D}{\frac{2}{3}r} = \frac{9}{8}(\frac{D}{r}) = \frac{9}{8}t$

8. a. 10 ft. by 15 ft.　**b.** 150 sq. ft.
$50 = 2(l + w) l = w + 5$

9. a. 5 units by 15 units
b. 75 square units
$l = 3w$
$40 = 2(l + w)$

10. 125 yd. by 175 yd.
$600 = 2(l + w)$
$w = l - 50$

11. The new area is 20% of the original area.
$A = lw$
$(.25l)(.80w) = .2(lw) = .20A$

12. a. 14 cm by 20 cm　**b.** 280 sq. cm
$w = .70l$
$68 = 2(w + l)$
$A = wl$

13. a. 20 cm by 28 cm
$l = 1.40w$
$560 = lw$

b. 96 cm
$P = 2(l + w)$

14. 20 units by 40 units
$P = 3l = 2(l + w)$
$800 = lw$

15. a. 6 cm by 17 cm　**b.** 46 cm
$P = 2(l + w)$
$w = P - 40$
$102 = lw$

16. 12 units by 24 units
$l = 2w$
$lw = 288$

17. a. 15 cm by 18 cm　**b.** 270 sq. cm

$l = w + 3$

$A = lw$

$A - 30 = (l - 2)w$

18. $84 = A = lw$

   a. 7 ft. by 12 ft. $l = w + 5$

   b. 48 sq. ft. $A = 84 - 36$

   c. 36 sq. ft. $A = [7 - 2(1\frac{1}{2})][12 - 2(1\frac{1}{2})]$

   d. 4 ft. by 9 ft. $7 - 2(1\frac{1}{2})$, $12 - 2(1\frac{1}{2})$

19. **a.** 40 ft.

     $A = 50(60) = 3,000$

     $3(3,000) = (50 + s)(60 + s)$

   b. 90 ft. by 100 ft.

     $40 + 50$; $40 + 60$

   c. 9,000 sq. ft.

     $90(100)$

20. **a.** 10 in. by 12 in. **b.** 6 in. by 8 in.

     $120 = lw$

     $48 = (l - 4)(w - 4)$

21. 9 in. by 14 in.

   $126 = lw$

   $46 = 2(l + w)$

22. $l = 3w$

   $80 + 2(l + w)$, so $w = 10$, $l = 30$

   a. 111 sq. cm

     $A = 3(10) + 3(30) - 3(3)$ OR

     $A = 3(7) + 3(27) + 3(3)$

   b. 7 cm by 27 cm

     $10 - 3$; $30 - 3$

23. $1\frac{1}{2}$ ft.

   $\dfrac{15(8)}{2} = 60$, so $(15 - 2b)(8 - 2b) = 60$

24. 280 if the neighbor's fence is along the width; 260 if the neighbor's fence is along the length

$72,000 = lw$; $l = w + 60$

$y = \dfrac{2l + w}{3}$ if the neighbor's fence is along the width;

$y = \dfrac{l + 2w}{3}$ if the neighbor's fence is along the length.

25. 15 meters by 17 meters

$l = w + 2$

$255 = lw$

26. (Draw a diagram.)

   a. 35 ft. by 70 ft.

     $l = 2w$

     $A = lw = 2,450$

   b. 29 ft. by $30\frac{1}{2}$ ft.

     $35 - 2(3)$; $\dfrac{70 - 3(3)}{2}$

   c. $884\frac{1}{2}$ sq. ft.

     $A = 29(30\frac{1}{2})$

   d. 681 sq. ft.

     $A = 2,450 - 2(884\frac{1}{2})$

27. $w_s = l_s - 4$

$l_b = 2w_b$

$A = lw$

$A_u = A_b - A_s$

$P = 2(l + w)$

   a. small, 6 in. by 10 in.

     large, 8 in. by 16 in.

     $A_u = 68$

   b. small, 9 in. by 13 in.;

     large, 13 in. by 26 in.

$A_u = 221$

$W_b = l_s$

c. small, 3 in. by 7 in.;
  large, 5 in. by 10 in.
  $A_u = 29$

$P_b - P_s = 10$

Notice that another set of answers, 33 in by 37 in for the small rectangle, and 25 in by 50 in for the large rectangle, checks out both for difference in perimeter and difference in area. However, the small rectangle doesn't fit inside the large one.

d. small, 4 in. by 8 in.;
  large, 11 in. by 22 in.
  $A_u = 210$

$W_b = l_s + 3$

e. small, 2 in. by 6 in.;
  large, 4 in. by 8 in.
  $A_u = 20$

$l_b = l_s + 2$

$w_b = w_s + 2$

f. small, 5 in. by 9 in.;
  large, 7 in. by 14 in.
  $A_u = 53$

$28 = 2(w_s + l_s)$

g. small, 2 in. by 6 in.;
  large, 8 in. by 16 in.
  $A_u = 116$

$l_b = 2(w_s + l_s)$

h. small, $5\frac{1}{7}$ in. by $9\frac{1}{7}$ in.;

  large, $6\frac{6}{7}$ in. by $13\frac{5}{7}$ in.

  $A_u = A_s$

  $w_s = \frac{3}{4} w_b$

i. small, 8 in. by 12 in.;
  large, 12 in. by 24 in.

$A_u = 2A_s$

$P_s = P_b - 32$

j. small, 28 in. by 32 in.;
  large, 32 in. by 64 in.
  $A_u = 6P_b$

$l_s = w_b$

k. small, 4 in. by 8 in.;
  large, 10 in. by 20 in.
  $A_u = 7P_s$

$w_b = l_s + 2$

28. $A = lw$
  $lw + (l + 2)(w + 1) = 286$
  $(l + 2)(w + 1) - lw = 34$

  a. 8 in. by 20 in. OR 10 in. by 16 in.

  b. 7 in. by 18 in. OR 9 in. by 14 in.

  c. 160 sq. in.   **d.** 126 sq in.

29. $lw = 576$
  a. 12 in. by 48 in.
    $(w - 3)(l + 16) = 576$

  b. 9 in. by 64 in.
    $(l + 3)w = 576 + 27$

  c. 8 in. by 72 in.
    $(w - 2)l = 576 - 144$

30. $lw = 576$
  a. 16 in. by 36 in.
    $l = w + 20$

  b. 18 in. by 32 in.
    $w = l - 14$

  c. 24 in. by 24 in.
    $l = w$

31. 15 units by 24 units
  $lw = 360$
  $(l + 1)(w + 1) = 400$

32. a. width, $3\sqrt{(21 + \pi)}$ in;

length, $12\sqrt{(21 + \pi)}$ in.

(That's about 14.74 in. for width, and about 58.96 in. for length.)

$A_D = \pi r^2 = 36\pi$

$A_r = lw$

$l = 4w$

$A_u = A_r - A_D = 756$

b. width, $39\frac{39\sqrt{7}}{7}$ in.;

length, $156\frac{156\sqrt{7}}{7}$ in.

(Same approximations.)

Using the work from part a,

$w^2 = 9(21 + 3\frac{1}{7})$.

l can be found the same way, but it's easier to take $l = 4w$.

33. $A = lw$

a. 3 ft.

$40(50) + 576 = (40 + 2s)(50 + 2s)$

b. 784 sq. ft.

$A = (40 + 8)(50 + 8) - 40(50)$

c. 4 ft.

$l = w + 10$

$192 = 2[(l + 2s) + (w + 2s)]$

$lw + 704 = (l + 2s)(w + 2s)$

(The building is 35 ft by 45 ft.)

d. 146 ft.

$648 = (l + 8)(w + 8) - lw$

$P = 2(l + w)$

e. 28 ft. by 42 ft.

$w = \frac{2}{3} l$

$wl + 800 = (w + 10)(l + 10)$

34. 44 kph

$D = rt$, average speed $= \dfrac{\text{sum of distances}}{\text{sum of times}}$

$D_1 = 40(3)$; $D_2 = 50(2)$

35. $t = \dfrac{D}{r}$; $r = \dfrac{D}{t}$

a = average speed $= \dfrac{\text{sum of distances}}{\text{sum of times}}$

$r_1 = 50$, $r_2 = 60$, $r_3 = 80$

(1) $a = \dfrac{D_1 + D_2}{t_1 + t_2}$

(2) $a = \dfrac{2(D_1 + D_2)}{t_1 + t_2 + t_3}$

a. (1) 55 kph; (2) $65\frac{5}{27}$ kph

$D_1 = 100$, $D_2 = 120$

b. (1) $54\frac{6}{11}$ kph; (2) $64\frac{32}{37}$ kph

$D_1 = 300$, $D_2 = 300$

c. (1) $54\frac{6}{61}$ kph; (2) $64\frac{224}{409}$ kph

$D_1 = 120$, $D_2 = 100$

36. $73\frac{1}{3}$ kph

$D = rt$; $r = \dfrac{D}{t}$

average speed $= \dfrac{\text{sum of distances}}{\text{sum of times}}$

Put D = half the total distance.

$t_1 = \dfrac{D}{60}$

$t_1 + t_2 = \dfrac{2D}{66}$

(Solve for t_2 and then apply the formula $r_2 = \dfrac{D}{t_2}$.)

37. a. 50 kph   **b.** 300 km

$D = 6r = 5(r + 10)$

38. $D = (3\frac{40}{60})(60) = 220$

a. $2\frac{3}{4}$ hour $t = \dfrac{220}{80}$

b. 88 kph $r = \dfrac{220}{2\frac{1}{2}}$

39. 2:15 p.m.

$D = 50t = 90(t - 1)$

Solve for t, convert to hours and minutes, and add to 12:00 noon.

40. from 72 seconds to 45 seconds

$D = rt$, so at 25 mph, $t =$

$$\frac{\frac{1}{2} \text{ mile}}{25 \text{ mph}} (3{,}600 \text{ seconds per hour}) =$$

72 seconds. At 40 mph, $t = \dfrac{\frac{1}{2} \text{ mile}}{40 \text{ mph}}$

$(3{,}600 \text{ seconds per hour}) = 45$ seconds.

41. $1{,}470 = (r + c)(3)$
$2{,}050 = (r - c)(5)$

a. 40 mph   **b.** 450 mph

42. $7\frac{1}{2}$ mph

$$3\left(\frac{1}{4}\right) = r\left(\frac{6}{60}\right)$$

43. 40 mph

$$100 = rt = (r + 8)\left(t - \frac{25}{60}\right)$$

44. a. 3mph **b.** 15 mph

$18 = (r - c)\left(1\frac{1}{2}\right)$
$36 = (r + c)(2)$

45. a. 60 kph **b.** 40 kph

$$D = rt = (r - 20)\left(\frac{3}{2}t\right)$$

46. a. 3 hours **b.** 24 km

$$D = 8t = 9\left(t - \frac{20}{60}\right)$$

47. $72\frac{1}{2}$ kph

$$D = 75(1) = 80\left(\frac{20}{60}\right) + r\left(\frac{40}{60}\right)$$

48. a. 1 hour

$$60t = 80\left(t - \frac{1}{4}\right)$$

b. 60 km
$D = 60(1)$

49. a. 15

$$t_A = \frac{30}{8} \; ; \; t_G = \frac{30}{10}$$
$$f = t_A - \frac{1}{2} - T_G$$

b. 2:30 p.m.

$D = 8t = 10\left(t - \frac{1}{2}\right)$. Solve for t, convert to hours and minutes, and add to 12:00 noon.

50. $D = rt = (r + 10)\left(t - \frac{1}{2}\right) =$
$(r - 10)\left(t + \frac{2}{3}\right)$

a. 70 kph **b.** 4 hours

c. 80 kph
$r = 70 + 10$

d. $3\frac{1}{2}$ hours

$$t = 4 - \frac{1}{2}$$

51. a. $27\frac{7}{9}$ mph **b.** $472\frac{2}{9}$ mph

$2{,}000 = (r - w)\left(4\frac{1}{2}\right) = (r + w)(4)$

52. a. 2 km

$$D = 30\left(\frac{2}{60}\right) + 40\frac{1\frac{1}{2}}{60}$$

b. $34\frac{2}{7}$ kph

$$r = \frac{2}{\frac{2}{60} + \frac{1\frac{1}{2}}{60}}$$

53. a. 48 kph **b.** $7\frac{1}{2}$ hours

$$360 = rt = (r + 2)(t - \frac{18}{60})$$

54. $106\frac{2}{3}$ kph

Put D = the length of one lap, T = total time, t = time taken for one lap at 80 kph. Then $t = \frac{D}{80}$, and $5D = 100T$, so $r = \frac{4D}{T - t}$.

55. $68\frac{4}{7}$ kph

$$D = 60t_1 = 80t_2;\ a = \frac{2D}{t_1 + t_2}$$

56. $34\frac{2}{7}$ kph

Put D = the distance covered on half of the slope. Then $D = rt = 40t_1 = 30t_2$ so $t_1 = \frac{3}{4}t_2$. Average rate =

$$\frac{\text{total distance}}{\text{total time}} = \frac{2D}{t_1 + t_2} = \frac{2(30t_2)}{\frac{3}{4}t_2 + t_2}$$

57. $32\frac{8}{11}$ kph

Put D = the distance covered on one-third of the slope. Then $D = 40t_1$ and $2D = 30t_2$ so $t_1 = \frac{3}{8}t_2$.

$$\text{Average rate} = \frac{\text{total distance}}{\text{total time}} = \frac{3D}{t_1 + t_2} = \frac{3(15t_2)}{\frac{3}{8}t_2 + t_2}$$

58. $27\frac{9}{13}$ kph

Put D = the distance covered on one-third of the slope. Then
$D = 40t_1 = 30t_2 = 20t_3$,

$$\text{Average rate} = \frac{\text{total distance}}{\text{total time}} = \frac{3D}{t_1 + t_2 + t_3} = \frac{3(20t_3)}{\frac{1}{2}t_3 + \frac{2}{3}t_3 + t_3}$$

59. $D = rt = (r + 8)(t - 1) = (r - 3\frac{1}{2})(t + \frac{1}{2})$

a. $11\frac{1}{2}$ hours **b.** 84 kph

c. 966 km

$$D = 84(11\frac{1}{2})$$

60. Put T = total time allotted = $\frac{2(\text{track length})}{120}$.

Put t_1 = time taken on first lap = $\frac{\text{track length}}{\text{rate on first lap}}$.

Put r = rate needed on second lap =
$$\frac{\text{track length}}{T - t_1}.$$

a. 180 mph

$$T = \frac{2(5)}{120}$$
$$t_1 = \frac{5}{90}$$
$$r = \frac{5}{T - t_1}$$

b. The car can no longer quality, regardless of its speed.

$$T = \frac{2(5)}{120}$$
$$t_1 = \frac{5}{60}$$
$$r = \frac{5}{T - t_1} = \frac{5}{0}$$

61. a. 120 miles **b.** 50 mph
If the cars started at the same time and traveled at the same rate, they met at the half-way point. So the distance from A to B = 2(60) = 120 miles. Then $r_A t_A =$ 120 – 35, and $r_A (t_A - 1) = 35$.

c. 110 miles **d.** $45\frac{5}{6}$ mph for A, 55 mph for B

On the return trip, $r_B t_B = 60$,

$\frac{5}{6} r_B t_B = D - 60$, so $D = 110$.

On the first trip, $\frac{5}{6} r_B (t_B + 1) =$

$D - 35$, $r_B t_B = 35$.

62. a. 7 min. 30 sec.

$t_A = \frac{5}{10}$ hr = 30 min

$t_B = \frac{5}{8}$ hr = $37\frac{1}{2}$ min

b. $\dfrac{150 \text{ minutes}}{\text{Alma's speed in mph}}$

$t_A = \frac{5}{r_A}$ hr = $\frac{300}{r_A}$ min

$t_B = \dfrac{5}{\frac{2}{3} r_A}$ hr = $\dfrac{450}{r_A}$ min

c. Alma will finish 11 min. 40 sec. before Belinda finishes.

$t_B = \frac{5}{6}$ hr = 50 min

$t_A = \frac{5}{9}$ hr = 33 min 20 sec

Difference = 45 min – 33 min 20 sec = 11 min 40 sec

d. They will tie if Alma's rate is 20 mph. Alma will win by $\dfrac{100}{r_A} - 5$ min. if her speed is less than 20 mph. Belinda will win by

$5 - \dfrac{100}{r_A}$ min. if Alma's speed is more than 20 mph.

$t_A = \frac{5}{r_A}$ hr = $\frac{300}{r_A}$ min

$t_B = \dfrac{5}{\frac{3}{4} r_A}$ hr = $\dfrac{400}{r_A}$ min

So $t_B - t_A = \dfrac{100}{r_A}$ min. So they will

tie if $\dfrac{100}{r_A} = 5$; Alma will win if

$\dfrac{100}{r_A} > 5$; Belinda will win if $\dfrac{100}{r_A} < 5$.

63. A won.

Put D = the one-way distance, r = rate in still water, t = time in still water. Then $D = rt$, and $2D = r(2t)$, so the total time for A was $2t = \dfrac{2D}{r}$

For B, $D = (r - c)t_u = (r + c)t_d$ and the

total time for B was $t_u + t_d =$

$\left(\dfrac{D}{r - c} + \dfrac{D}{r + c} \right) = D \left(\dfrac{1}{r - c} + \dfrac{1}{r + c} \right) = \dfrac{2Dr}{r^2 - c^2}$

Now $r^2 - c^2 < r^2$, so $\dfrac{2Dr}{r^2 - c^2} > \dfrac{2Dr}{r^2} = \dfrac{2D}{r} = 2t$.

Therefore, $t_u + t_d > 2t$, and so B took

more time than A.

PERCENTS AND WORK RATES

The problems in this section are, by nature, more difficult than the problems in the other sections dealing with specific categories. Consequently, while the problems at the beginning of either of the categories in this section are among the easiest of their type, they are still more difficult than the beginning problems in the other sections mentioned.

A hand calculator is helpful for most of these problems and is essential for some of the investment problems, unless the student knows how to work with logarithms.

While solving the problems, I graded them at one of nine difficulty levels— three levels each at easy, medium, and hard—according to how difficult I thought a student would find it to set up the needed equations and to solve the equations once they were set up.

Whereas a straightforward problem of solving $A = 10,000(1.04)^{10}$ would be hard without either logs or a calculator, it would be easy with logs, ridiculously easy with a calculator capable of multiplying by a constant, and of medium difficulty if numbers had to be entered in the calculator each time a multiplication was to be performed.

On the other hand, a problem such as $900 = 500(1 + \frac{r}{4})^{20}$, where an answer accurate to one decimal place is wanted, would be impossible without a working knowledge of logarithms, but it would not otherwise be particularly difficult.

In grading the difficulty, then, I decided to assume that a student would have a hand calculator capable of multiplying by a constant but not capable of computing logs. Then (assuming the problem was stated in a way to make the required equation obvious), the example two paragraphs above was graded as easy, and the example one paragraph above was graded as medium.

When a student was assumed to have to use logs, I used a four-place log table. Consequently, if the student uses a table accurate to a different number of places, the answer may be slightly different than mine.

Once an answer using logs is obtained, the accuracy can be checked on a hand calculator. The accuracy should be checked if one really wants to know the answer to such a problem, for dividing a log by 20 and then multiplying a final answer by 4 (such as would be necessary in the example three paragraphs above) can lead to an erroneous conclusion if one is actually trying to decide what rate of interest is being earned.

Problems involving interest are somewhat difficult for high school students for various reasons.

First, the students don't seem to realize that interest is a fee charged for the use of money, and they might benefit from the following examples:

(1) Brown borrows money from a loan company. The loan company charges a fee (interest) for the use of their money.

(2) Green charges merchandise on an account at a department store. If the charge account is paid when due, the store does not add anything extra to the account, thus allowing Green the use of the money (the unpaid account) without a fee. But if the account is not paid when due, then the store adds a fee (interest or a "finance charge") for the use of their money.

(3) Black puts money into a savings account at a bank. The bank pays Black a fee (interest) for the use of Black's money.

(4) A store arranges to accept BANK charge cards for merchandise it sells its customers. The customer charges merchandise on a BANK card. The store turns in the charge slip to BANK and gets its money for the merchandise. But then BANK has paid out money to the store. BANK charges the store a fee for the use of this money and then takes the responsibility of collecting from the customer. If the customer pays BANK when the account is due, no further fee is charged. If the customer is late in paying the account, BANK adds a fee (interest or "finance charge") to the account for the extra length of time the customer is using BANK's money.

(5) The Johnsons buy a $30,000 house, paying $5,000 down and signing a $25,000 mortgage. The mortgage company charges the Johnsons a fee (interest) for the use of its money. For as long as part of the $25,000 remains unpaid, the Johnsons are still using some of the mortgage company's money and must continue to pay them for the use of their money, but this fee (interest) decreases as the amount of money owed decreases.

(6) Same deal as (5), except the Johnsons sign a $25,000 land contract with the seller instead of a $25,000 mortgage with a mortgage company. Now the Johnsons are using the seller's money and must pay a fee (interest) to the seller for the use of this money.

Once students understand exactly what "interest" is, they still have trouble understanding what is meant by "compound interest," and it doesn't seem to make it any clearer to them when we tell them that the compound interest is "interest on interest." Perhaps the following examples will help clarify the concept for the students:

(1) Black puts $1,000 into a 6% savings account at a bank. At the end of the first quarter, the bank pays a $15 fee (interest) into Black's account. Black leaves the whole $1,015 in the account, and the bank is now using $1,015 of Black's money. At the end of the next quarter, the bank pays $15.23 (i.e., 1.5% of $1,015) as an interest fee, making Black's total account $1,030.23. At the end of the third quarter, the bank pays $15.45 as an interest fee, making Black's total account $1,045.68. At

the end of the fourth quarter, the bank pays $15.69 into the account, making the total $1,061.37. And so on. The point is, of course, that the bank is paying interest on all money in the account, and that included previous interest. In other words the bank is paying interest on interest—i.e., compound interest.

(2) The Joneses charge $500 on their BANK card at the beginning of a billing period and do not pay the account when BANK bills them for it. BANK adds $1\frac{1}{2}$%, $7.50, as a finance charge and bills them the following month for $507.50. (To keep the example simple, we'll assume no further BANK charges.) The Joneses again fail to pay the account, and BANK adds $1\frac{1}{2}$% of $507.50, $7.61, to the account, making the total due $515.11. The extra 11¢ was, of course, interest on the $7.50 interest owed from the preceding month, so BANK is charging compound interest.

Now even though the students will understand the concept of compound interest from examples such as those above, they will not see why the formula $A = \$1,000(1.015)^4$ should tell them the amount in Black's savings account at the end of four quarters. (The formula computes to $A = \$1,061.36$. The difference of 1¢ between this result and the result of (1) above is because the bank made an entry each quarter, rounding the current result to the nearest whole cent.)

It helps here to show them the following:

$a =$ $1,000 = Black's deposit

$b =$ .015(a) = bank's first deposit to Black's account. The account now has $a + b$ in it.

$c =$ .015($a + b$) = bank's second deposit to Black's account. The account now has $a + b + c$ in it.

$d =$ .015($a + b + c$) = bank's third deposit to Black's account. The account now has $a + b + c + d$ in it.

$e =$ .015($a + b + c + d$) = bank's fourth deposit to Black's account. The account now has $a + b + c + d + e$ in it.

Now we compute $a + b + c + d + e$:

$a =$ $1,000

$b =$ .015($1,000)

$a + b =$ $1,000(1 + .015) = $1,000(1.015)

$c =$ .015($1,000)(1.015)

$a + b + c =$ $1,000(1.015) + .015($1,000)(1.015)

= $1,000(1.015)(1 + .015) = $1,000(1.015)^2

$d =$ .015($1,000)(1.015)^2

$a + b + c + d =$ $1,000(1.015)^2 + .015($1,000)(1.015)^2

= $1,000(1.015)^2(1 + .015) = $1,000(1.015)^3

$e =$ .015($1,000)(1.015)^3
$a + b + c + d + e =$ $1,000(1.015)^3 + .015($1,000)(1.015)^3
= $1,000(1.015)^3(1 + .015) = $1,000(1.015)^4, thus giving us the desired result.

While we're at it, we can ask the students to notice several things about the above computations:

(1) The sum of all entries in the account, $a + b + c + d + e$, was the A of the formula being tested, so $A =$ $1,000(1.015)^4.

(2) The initial deposit of $1,000 was not used at all, except as a constant. It could have been any amount of principal invested, say P, and it would still have been P at the end of the computations. So we can substitute P for $1,000 to make the formula more general: $A = P(1.015)^4$.

(3) In every case, we got 1.015 from 1 + .015. The rate of .015 could have been any rate, say r. So we can make the formula even more general:

$$A = P(1 + r)^4.$$

(4) Finally, the exponent was 4 because we computed the amount after 4 interest periods. The exponent was 1 after the first period, 2 after the second, and 3 after the third. It could in fact be any number of interest periods, say n, and we would have the general formula given at the beginning of the section, $A = P(1 + r)^n$. (If your students have studied mathematical induction, ask them to prove this formula.)

Granted, the discussion and proof about interest suggested above will take a full class period, but the time spent will pay off in giving the students understanding and confidence in solving problems about compound interest.

Even with such understanding, however, it will probably not occur to the students, unless it is pointed out to them, that the r in the formula doesn't have to be interest. It can be any kind of appreciation in value that is a fixed rate.

Example:

(1) Gold has appreciated in value 11% each year for the past ten years. If

$2,000 was invested in gold ten years ago, how much is the investment worth now?

[Answer: $A = \$2,000(1.11)^{10} = \$5,678.84.$]

(2) Each year for the past six years, land that Larkspur bought six years ago for $4,000 has been worth 15% more than it was the year before. How much is it worth now?

[Answer: $A = \$4,000(1.15)^6 = \$9,252.24.$]

(3) The current rate of inflation is 4.5%. If this rate continues, how much money will it take in fifteen years to pay for something that costs $1,000 now?

[Answer: $A = \$1,000(1.045)^{15} = \$1,935.28.$]

Incidentally, most high school students don't understand what inflation is. They've heard the term, but the concept is vague. While they may understand that prices rise "because of inflation," they also know that wages rise for the same reason, and they usually have the idea that they don't have to pay much attention to it because everything evens out in the end.

It is helpful to have a discussion of income in terms of purchasing power, with the emphasis on the problem of the retired person who is living on a fixed income. (Choose a fixed monthly income, and choose a budget that includes food, clothing, medical expenses not covered by Medicaid or Medicare, taxes, rent, utilities, transportation expenses, and so on. Figure out what each budgeted item will cost in five years at the current inflation rate. Ask what will have to be eliminated from the retired person's spending, since

the income did not also rise.)

Students often have trouble with problems that give a total amount invested and ask for the amount invested at each of two rates of interest. It might be helpful to point out that such problems are analogous to coin problems.

Example:

Robin invests $5,000, part at 5% and the rest at 10%. The yearly income from these investments is $340. How much is invested at each rate?

The equations needed for this problem are

$$f + t = 5000$$
$$.05f + .10t = 340$$

Notice that the same system of equations would solve this problem: Robin has 5,000 nickels and dimes that total $340. How many each of nickels and dimes are there?

In either case, the answer is $f = 3,200$, $t = 1,800$. (If the interest rates are something like 6% and 8%, one can always think in terms of 6¢ and 8¢ coins.)

Similar comments apply to problems involving discounts given or percents of profit or whatever. It is sometimes effective to stress to the students the mathematical sameness of all such problems and to prove it by pointing out that the equations don't know whether the solver is trying to find numbers of coins, amounts of investments, amounts of merchandise sold or bought, or whatever.

For problems involving rates of work, certain trouble spots should be anticipated and circumvented. Some of these are discussed below.

Put A = the number of hours Ann

needs to do a job, B = the number of hours Bob needs to do the job, h = the number of hours the job takes when they work on it together. Then

$$\frac{1}{A} + \frac{1}{B} = \frac{1}{h}$$

is the amount of work done in one hour. Now suppose we are told that when Ann works at only half of her usual efficiency, the job takes two hours more. It might seem natural to alter the equation to

$$\frac{1}{\frac{1}{2}A} + \frac{1}{B} = \frac{1}{h+2},$$

but the first term would be wrong. If Ann usually takes twenty hours for a job but is working only at half her usual rate, she will take forty hours, not ten hours—i.e., $2A$ not $\frac{1}{2}A$—to do the job. So the equation should be $\frac{1}{2}(\frac{1}{A}) + \frac{1}{B} = \frac{1}{h+2}$. Similarly, if Ann works twice as fast as Bob, we have $A = \frac{1}{2}B$, not $A = 2B$, since it will take her only half as long as Bob to do the job.

Along this same line, if Ann takes 20 hours to do a job, and if Bob works 25% faster than Ann, it is tempting to take 25% of 20 = 5 and conclude that Bob takes 20 – 5 = 15 hours for the job. But the equation needed for this problem is

$$\frac{1}{B} = 1.25(\frac{1}{A}) = 1.25(\frac{1}{20}) = \frac{5}{4}(\frac{1}{20}) = \frac{1}{16},$$

and we see that Bob takes 16, not 15, hours to do the job.

This concept might be easier for the students to grasp if we let A = Ann's rate of work (i.e., $\frac{1}{20}$ of the job done in one hour) and let B = Bob's rate of work. Then

$B = 1.25A$, which is certainly clearer than the equation above, and so $B = \frac{5}{4}(\frac{1}{20}) = \frac{1}{16}$.

Also, if it takes Ann and Bob ten hours to do the job working together, we have a choice of two main ways to set up an equation for this. Whereas

$$\frac{1}{A} + \frac{1}{B} = \frac{1}{10}$$

says that one-tenth of the job will be done in one hour,

$$10(\frac{1}{A} + \frac{1}{B}) = 1 \text{ OR } \frac{10}{A} + \frac{10}{B} = 1$$

says that the whole job will be done in ten hours. This second form is useful in sorting out our thoughts when we want to express something like, "If Ann works for three hours and Bob works for five hours, then the job is half done." We can write

$$\frac{3}{A} + \frac{5}{B} = \frac{1}{2}$$

to express the statement. And of course if we want to put A, B = Ann's and Bob's rates of work, we can write

$$3A + 5B = \frac{1}{2},$$

but then we have to remember when we find the A and B values that the numbers we really want are $\frac{1}{A}$ and $\frac{1}{B}$.

Alternatively, we could put A, B = the numbers of hours Ann and Bob need to do the job alone, but also put $a = \frac{1}{A}$, $b = \frac{1}{B}$. This method is sometimes preferred by students who dislike working with $\frac{1}{A}$ and $\frac{1}{B}$ in the equations. At the same time, such students may have trouble realizing exactly what a and b stand for in terms of physical realities and so not recognize that the equation needed in the above example is $3a + 5b = \frac{1}{2}$.

It is always possible, of course, to set up the system needed in terms of $\frac{1}{A}$ and $\frac{1}{B}$ and then make substitutions of a and b before solving the system, thus making the system both easy to set up and easy to solve.

Note: " * " following a problem number indicates that the use of a calculator or logarithms is essential. "L" indicates the use of logarithms is essential.

PERCENTS AND WORK RATES DETAILED SOLUTIONS

1. 24. $.25t = 6$

2. $80. $1.25c = 100$

3. $225. $.60g = 135$

4. $30. $.70p = 21$

5. 2,000. $.15t = 300$

6. 3 inches. $3.5b = 10.5$

7. 110. $.40t = 44$

8. **a.** $150. $.78g = 117$

   b. $10.50. $.07(\$150)$

   c. $22.50. $.15(\$150)$

9. **a.** $13,505. $1.10s = 14,855.50$

   b. $1,350.50. $.10(\$13,505)$ OR $14,855.50 - \$13,505.00$

10. **a.** $19,000. $.05t = 950$

    b. $25,000. $.95t = 23,750$

    c. $1,250. $.05(\$25,000)$ OR $25,000 - \$23,750$

11. $211.30. $.90g = 190.17$

12. 60. $.20d + .30d = 30$

13. **a.** $2,000. $.75s = 1500$

    b. $6,000. $.25s = 1500$

14. $102.47. $.98a = 100.42$

15. $1.79 a pound. $.70a = 1.25$

16. **a.** $600
    $n + b = 1100$
    $n = 1.20b$

    b. $500. $i = 2(.10)(2,500)$ OR $i = 3,000 - 2,500$

17. 4. $.95b(500) = 1900$

18. **a.** $11.75 $1.07c = 12.57$

    b. 47¢ $t = .04(11.75)$

    c. 35¢ $t = .03(11.75)$

19. **a.** $15,000 $2(.10a) = 3000$

    b. $2,500 $a + 2(.10)a = 3000$

    c. $500 $i = 2(.10)(2500)$ OR $i = 3000 - 2500$

20. **a.** $33,500. $.92s - 350 - 30,000 = 470$

    b. $2,680. $.08(\$33,500)$

21. **a.** $400. $.665g - 5 - 25 = 236$

    b. $28. $t = .07(400)$

    c. $80. $t = .20(400)$

    d. $20. $t = .05(400)$

    e. $6. $t = .015(400)$

22. 8%. $3000(.06) + 4000(\frac{r}{100}) = 500$

23. **a.** $35. **b.** $10.
    $g + e = 45$ $e = g + 25$

c. $42. $s = 1.20(35)$

d. $13. $s = 1.30(10)$

24.* $3,221.02. $A = 2,000(1.10)^5$

25.* **a.** $5,450 $A = 5,000 + .09(5,000)$

b. $5,450 $A = 5,000(1.09)^1$

c. $5,460.13 $A = 5,000(1.045)^2$

d. $5,465.42 $A = 5,000(1.0225)^4$

e. $5,469.03 $A = 5,000(1.0075)^{12}$

f. $5,470.81 $A = 5,000(1.00025)^{360}$

26.* $14,802.44. $A = 10,000(1.04)^{10}$

27.* **a.** $1,300 $A = 1,000 + 5(.06)(1,000)$

b. $1,338.23 $A = 1,000(1.06)^5$

c. $1,343.92 $A = 1,000(1.03)^{10}$

d. $1,346.86 $A = 1,000(1.015)^{20}$

e. $1,348.85 $A = 1,000(1.005)^{60}$

28.* **a.** $2,000. $2,320 = P + 2(.08)P$

b. $1,989.03 $P = \dfrac{2,320}{1.08^2}$

c. $1,983.15 $P = \dfrac{2,320}{1.04^4}$

d. $1,980.10 $P = \dfrac{2,320}{1.02^8}$

29. **a.** 50. $r + w = t$
$r = w + 30$
$.80t = r$

b. 40. $.80(50)$

c. 10. $50 - 40$ OR $40 - 30$

30. $\dfrac{1}{2} \cdot \dfrac{.75n}{1.25d} = \dfrac{3}{10}$ (Solve for $\dfrac{n}{d}$.)

31.* $4,563.87. $10,000 = P(1.04)^{20}$

32. $3,500 at 8%, $6,500 at 10%
$.08e + .10t = 930$
$.10e + .08t = 930 - 60$

33. **a.** $35
$.98(100)s - 1.02[100(30)] = 370$

b. $70. $c = .02(35)(100)$

34. $2,000 at 6%, $4,000 at 9%
$s + n = 6,000$
$.06s + .09n = .08(6,000)$

35. $2,500 at 10%, $1,500 at 15%
$t + f = 4,000$
$.10t + .15f = 475$

36. $7,750
$1,080 + .22x = 1,465$
income = $x + 6,000$

37. $4,000 at 6%, $6,000 at 7%
$s + v = 10,000$
$.06s + .07v = 660$

38. $e + t = 10,000$
a. $2,500 at 8%, $7,500 at 10%
$.08e + .10t = 950$

b. $7,500 at 8%, $2,500 at 10%
$.08e + .10t = .085(10,000)$

39. **a.** $25,896.75. $.04t = 1,035.87$

b. $996.03. $1.04s = 1,035.87$

c. $39.84. $x = .04(996.03)$ OR
$x = 1,035.87 - 996.03$

40. $A + B = 10,000$
a–b.
$.08A + .12B = c$
a. $3,000 of A, $7,000 of B
$c = 1,080$

b. $5,500 of A, $4,500 of B
$c = 980$

c. 10. $.08(7,000) + p(3,000) = 860$

d. 9. $.08(2,000) + p(8,000) = 880$

41. a. detergent, $188; meat, $162
$.75m + .95d = 300.10$
$m + d = 350$

  b. detergent, $178.60; meat, $121.50
$d = .95(188)$
$m = .75(162)$

42. a. $18 for the item discounted 15%,
$22 for the item discounted 20%.
$f + t = 40$
$.85f + .80t = 32.90$

  b. $15.30 for the item discounted
15%, $17.60 for the item
discounted 20%.
$.85(18)$ and $.80(22)$

43. 3 pounds for $1 or 34¢ a pound. (If
it's $33\frac{1}{3}$¢ a pound, the store will
charge 34¢ a pound.)
$90\%(50 \text{ lbs}) = 45$ saleable lbs
$12 = .80(45s)$

44. a. $4,800 and $7,200.
$b + s = 12,000$
$b = \frac{3}{2}s$

  b. 10% on $4,800; $7\frac{1}{2}$% on $7,200.
$4,800(\frac{r}{100}) + 7,200[(\frac{3}{4})\frac{r}{100}] =$
$1,020$

  c. $480 on $4,800, $540 on
$7,200

45. a. $30 for the pair discounted 40%,
$20 for the pair discounted
25%.
$f + t = 50$
$.60f + .75t = 33$

  b. $18 for the pair discounted 40%,
$15 for the pair discounted 25%.
$.60(\$30)$ and $.75(\$20)$

46. a. $3 $t = 200, d = 570$

  b. $2.50 $t = 460, d = 1,092.50$

  c. $\$\frac{d}{.95t}$ $.25t(.80p) + .75tp = d$

47. a. $46.60 $1.03t + 52 = 100$

  b. $1.40
$.03(\$46.60)$ OR $48 – $46.60

48.* a. $1,790.85 $A = 1,000(1.06)^{10}$

  b. $558.39 $1,000 = P(1.06)^{10}$

49.* a. $1,814.02 $A = 1,000(1 + \frac{.06}{4})^{10(4)}$,
so $A = 1,000(1.015)^{40}$

  b. $551.26. $1,000 = P(1.015)^{40}$

50. $400 to A, $10,400 to B.
$.60A + .65B = 7,000$
$.65A + .60B = 7,000 – 500$

51. L a. 8%. $(1 + r)^5 = \frac{1,469.33}{1,000}$

  b. 7.8%. $(1 + \frac{r}{2})^{10} = \frac{1,469.33}{1,000}$

(Checking the answer of 7.8% in the
equation gives 1,466.07, rather than
1,469.33, whereas 7.9% gives 1,473.14.)

  c. $(1 + \frac{r}{4})^{20} = \frac{1,469.33}{1,000}$

(This is a good example of the inaccu-
racy that can result from multiplying or
dividing a log by a relatively large number—20, in this case. A four-place log
table gives an answer of 8%, and a five-
place table gives an answer of 7.6%,
neither of which is accurate. Actually, the
rate is about 7.77%.)

52. * (This is a hard problem!)

    a. $3,221.02. $A = 2,000(1.10)^5$

    b. $527.59; $2,637.95. Interest will be computed at the end of each year, and then a payment will be made, starting the new year with a new balance. The process will be repeated each year for five years, thus resulting in the equation (where p = the amount of the payment to be made)

year 1   year 2   year 3 year 4 year 5

$\{[(\{[2,000(1.10) - p](1.10) - p\}(1.10 - p)(1.10) - p](1.10) - p\} = 0.$

Then $2,000(1.10)^5 - p(1.10)^4 - p(1.10)^3 - p(1.10)^2 - p(1.10) - p = 0.$

So, $2,000(1.10)^5 = p[1.10^4 + 1.10^3 + 1.10^2$

$+ 1.10 + 1]$, and $2,000(1.10)^5 = p \cdot \dfrac{1.10^5 - 1}{1.10 - 1}.$

So $p = \dfrac{2,000(1.10)^5(.10)}{1.10^5 - 1} =$

$\dfrac{2,000(1.61051)(.10)}{.61051} = \dfrac{322.102}{.61051} = 527.59,$

where the last three "=" are approximate. (If we work out the figures year by year, she will make four payments of $527.59 and one of $527.63. If she makes four payments of $527.60, the final payment will be $527.56, so either way the final payment is 4¢ different than the other four payments.)

    c. $42.49; $2,549.40. Following the reasoning of part b above, we see that the equation to be solved will be

$$p = \dfrac{2,000\left(1 + \frac{.10}{12}\right)^{60}\left(\frac{.10}{12}\right)}{\left(1 + \frac{.10}{12}\right)^{60} - 1}$$

$= \text{(approx.)}\ \dfrac{2,000(1.64530893398)\left(.008\frac{1}{3}\right)}{.64530893398}$

$= \text{(approx.)}\ 42.49.$

(The figures are given through the courtesy of my 12-digit calculator.)

53. * (This is a hard problem!)

    a. $680,000. 17($40,000)

    b. $341,745.25. This is like problem **52b.** Here,

$40,000 = p = \dfrac{A(1.09)^{17}(.09)}{1.09^{17} - 1}$, so

$A = \dfrac{40,000(1.09^{17} - 1)}{1.09^{17}(.09)} = \$341,745.25.$

    c. $1,011.43. He will put the first amount into the fund at the end of his 22nd year and continue through the end of his 61st year a total of 40 deposits. Between the time of the deposit and the time of his 62nd birthday, the first deposit will earn interest for 39 years, the second for 38 years,…, the 39th for 1 year, and the 40th for 0 years, so we have $341,745.25 = D(1.09^{39} + 1.09^{38} +$

$…1.09^2 + 1.09 + 1) = \dfrac{D(1.09^{40} - 1)}{1.09 - 1},$

and so $D = \dfrac{341,745.25(.09)}{1.09^{40} - 1} =$

$1,011.43.$

    d. $281,599.55 a year

$A = 40,000(1.05)^{40} = \$281,599.55$

    e. The fund will need $2,405,541; and to have this amount, Yoshio should deposit $7,119.46 each year. (See part **b**.)

$A = \dfrac{281{,}599.55(1.09^{17} - 1)}{1.09^{17}(.09)} = \$2{,}405{,}541.00.$

(See part **c**.) $D = \dfrac{2{,}405{,}541(.09)}{1.09^{40} - 1} = \$7{,}119.46.$

[Whereas $1,011.43 is a relatively small amount to expect Yoshio to save each year (out of a $40,000 yearly salary) toward a retirement fund, $7,119.46 is not. You might point out to the students that Yoshio's salary, too, should be rising with inflation, and a $40,000 salary now will be a $281,599.55 salary in 40 years (at the 5% rate). Ask them if Yoshio could take care of inflation by simply depositing $1,011.43(1.05) the first year, $1,011.43(1.05)^2 the second year, and so on, and have it work out the same way. (The answer is no.)]

54. The easy way is to figure it takes 8 masons × 15 days = 120 mason-days to do the job, and then divide by the given (in each problem part) number of masons to get the number of days. The algebraic way is to figure that the number of days needed and the number of masons needed are inversely proportional and set up the equation $k = md$, computing $k = 120$ from the beginning information, and then setting up:

a. 12 days. $120 = 10d$

b. 30 days. $120 = 4d$

c. 40 days. $120 = 3d$

d. $7\frac{1}{2}$ days. $120 = 16d$

55. $R = kr^2$

$150 = k(3^2)$, so $k = \dfrac{150}{9} = \dfrac{50}{3}$

a. $266\frac{2}{3}$ gal. a sec. $R = \left(\dfrac{50}{3}\right)(4^2)$

b. $66\frac{2}{3}$ gal. a sec. $R = \left(\dfrac{50}{3}\right)(2^2)$

c. $416\frac{2}{3}$ gal. a sec. $R = \left(\dfrac{50}{3}\right)(5^2)$

d. $337\frac{1}{2}$ gal. a sec. $R = \left(\dfrac{50}{3}\right)\left(\dfrac{9}{2}\right)^2$

56. 24 days. $\dfrac{1}{H} + \dfrac{1}{J} = \dfrac{1}{6}$; $H = 8$

57. 12 minutes. $\dfrac{1}{4} - \dfrac{1}{6} = \dfrac{1}{m}$

58. 24 days. $\dfrac{1}{12} + \dfrac{1}{d} = \dfrac{1}{8}$

59. 15 hours for Laura, 30 hours for Marta.

$L = \dfrac{1}{2}M$

$\dfrac{1}{L} + \dfrac{1}{M} = \dfrac{1}{10}$

60. $312\frac{1}{2}$ gal. a min. through the smaller pipe, $437\frac{1}{2}$ gal. a min. through the larger pipe

$g = 1.40s$

$20(g + s) = 15{,}000$

61. 15 days for Ann, $22\frac{1}{2}$ days for Freda.

$\dfrac{1}{F} + \dfrac{1}{A} = \dfrac{1}{9}$

$\dfrac{1}{F} = \dfrac{2}{3}\left(\dfrac{1}{A}\right)$

62. 84 hours for Jeff, 60 hours for Ken.

$J = 1.40K$

$\dfrac{1}{J} + \dfrac{1}{K} = \dfrac{1}{35}$

63. **a.** 8 days. $\dfrac{1}{12} + \dfrac{1}{24} = \dfrac{1}{w}$

b. 6 days. Jai does $\dfrac{3}{12} = \dfrac{1}{4}$ of the job, leaving $\dfrac{3}{4}$ to do. $\dfrac{3}{4}$ of 8 = 6.

c. 7 days. Peter does $\dfrac{3}{24} = \dfrac{1}{8}$ of the job, leaving $\dfrac{7}{8}$ to do. $\dfrac{7}{8}$ of 8 = 7.

d. 11 days. Jai does $\dfrac{2}{12} = \dfrac{1}{6}$ of the job alone. Jai and Peter do $\dfrac{3}{8}$ of the job together. Then Peter has $1 - \left(\dfrac{1}{6} + \dfrac{3}{8}\right) = \dfrac{11}{24}$ of the job to do. $\dfrac{11}{24}$ of 24 = 11.

Alternatively, equations for **b–d** could be set up as follows:

63. **b.** $\dfrac{3}{12} + d\left(\dfrac{1}{12} + \dfrac{1}{24}\right) = 1$

c. $\dfrac{3}{24} + d\left(\dfrac{1}{12} + \dfrac{1}{24}\right) = 1$

d. $\dfrac{2}{12} + 3\left(\dfrac{1}{12} + \dfrac{1}{24}\right) + \dfrac{d}{24} = 1$

64. 10 hours for Karl, 40 hours for Louis.
$\dfrac{1}{K} + \dfrac{1}{L} = \dfrac{1}{8}$
$\dfrac{1}{2}\left(\dfrac{1}{K}\right) + 2\left(\dfrac{1}{L}\right) = \dfrac{1}{10}$

65. 36 hours for Carole, 45 hours for Katherine.
$\dfrac{1}{C} + \dfrac{1}{K} = \dfrac{1}{20}$

$\dfrac{1}{C} = 1.25\left(\dfrac{1}{K}\right)$

66. **a.** 10 days for Jim, 15 days for Frank, 30 days for Tony.
$\dfrac{1}{J} + \dfrac{1}{F} = \dfrac{1}{6}$
$\dfrac{1}{J} + \dfrac{1}{T} = \dfrac{1}{7\frac{1}{2}} = \dfrac{2}{15}$
$\dfrac{1}{T} + \dfrac{1}{F} = \dfrac{1}{10}$

b. 5 days. $\dfrac{1}{10} + \dfrac{1}{15} + \dfrac{1}{30} = \dfrac{1}{d}$

67. $H = 9$, $C = 6$, $S = 10$

a. 15 minutes. $\dfrac{1}{6} - \dfrac{1}{10} = \dfrac{1}{m}$

b. 90 minutes. $\dfrac{1}{9} - \dfrac{1}{10} = \dfrac{1}{m}$

c. $3\frac{3}{5}$ minutes. $\dfrac{1}{9} + \dfrac{1}{6} = \dfrac{1}{m}$

d. $5\frac{5}{8}$ minutes. $\dfrac{1}{9} + \dfrac{1}{6} - \dfrac{1}{10} = \dfrac{1}{m}$

68. $5\frac{2}{5}$ hours. $\dfrac{1}{N} = \dfrac{2}{3}\left(\dfrac{1}{10}\right) = \dfrac{1}{15}$
$\dfrac{1}{10} + h\left(\dfrac{1}{10} + \dfrac{1}{15}\right) = 1$

69. **a.** 16 hours. Letitia does half the job in 8 hours, so $L = 2(8) = 16$, or if we want an equation, $L - 8 = \dfrac{1}{2}L$.

b–c **b.** 5 hours. **c.** $26\frac{2}{3}$ hours. Since it takes the girls 10 hours to do the whole job, it will take them 5 hours to do half the job, so $\dfrac{1}{8} + \dfrac{1}{\frac{1}{2}J} = \dfrac{1}{5}$, OR $\dfrac{1}{16} + \dfrac{1}{J} = \dfrac{1}{10}$.

70. 20 days for Dave, 10 days for Joe, 40 days for Tom

$$\frac{1}{T} + \frac{1}{J} = 8$$

$$\frac{1}{T} + \frac{1}{D} = \frac{1}{13\frac{1}{3}}$$

$$\frac{1}{J} + \frac{1}{D} = \frac{1}{6\frac{2}{3}}$$

71. $2\frac{6}{7}$ hours

$$\frac{1}{B} = \frac{3}{4}\left(\frac{1}{K}\right) = \frac{3}{4}\left(\frac{1}{9}\right) = \frac{1}{12}$$

$$\frac{4}{9} + h\left(\frac{1}{9} + \frac{1}{12}\right) = 1$$

72. a–d. $L = 20, \; S = 30, \; D = 40$

a. 12 minutes. $\dfrac{1}{20} + \dfrac{1}{30} = \dfrac{1}{m}$

b. 40 minutes. $\dfrac{1}{20} - \dfrac{1}{40} = \dfrac{1}{m}$

c. 2 hours. $\dfrac{1}{30} - \dfrac{1}{40} = \dfrac{1}{m}$

d. $17\frac{1}{7}$ minutes. $\dfrac{1}{20} + \dfrac{1}{30} - \dfrac{1}{40} = \dfrac{1}{m}$

e–h. $L = 20, \dfrac{1}{20} + \dfrac{1}{S} = \dfrac{1}{15}, \dfrac{1}{S} - \dfrac{1}{D} = \dfrac{1}{240}$

e. 1 hour. $\dfrac{1}{S} = \dfrac{1}{15} - \dfrac{1}{20}$

f. 1 hour 20 min. $\dfrac{1}{D} = \dfrac{1}{60} - \dfrac{1}{240}$

g. $26\frac{2}{3}$ min. OR 26 min. 40 sec.

$$\frac{1}{20} - \frac{1}{80} = \frac{1}{m}$$

h. $18\frac{6}{13}$ min. OR 18 min. $27\frac{9}{13}$ sec

$$\frac{1}{20} + \frac{1}{60} - \frac{1}{80} = \frac{1}{m}$$

73. (This is a hard problem!)
    a. Lyle 18 hrs., Theresa 36 hrs. Put
       h = the number of hours

ordinarily needed to do the job if Lyle and Theresa worked together—i.e., the number of hours needed if the 25% savings in efficiency were not in effect. Then we would have $\dfrac{1}{L} + \dfrac{1}{T} = \dfrac{1}{h}$, and so $T = \dfrac{hL}{L - h}$.

Lyle needed 6 hours to do $\dfrac{1}{3}$ of the job when he worked alone, so it takes him 18 hours to do the whole job alone, and we will have $T = \dfrac{18h}{18 - h}$.

It took 6 hours of working together to do $\dfrac{2}{3}$ of the job, and this was at a 25% savings in efficiency, so $6 = \dfrac{2}{3}(.75h)$, and so $h = 12$. Therefore, $T = \dfrac{12(18)}{18 - 12} = 36$.

To check, we take $\dfrac{1}{L} + \dfrac{1}{T} = \dfrac{1}{18} + \dfrac{1}{36} = \dfrac{1}{12}$ implying it takes 12 hours to do the job together with no savings of time in increased efficiency. Then 75% of 12 = 9 hours to do the job when the time is reduced by 25%. Then $\dfrac{2}{3}$ of 9 = 6 hours to do $\dfrac{2}{3}$ of the job together, and this is what we were given.

b. 16 hours. See discussion in **a** above.
    $.75h = 6$, so $h = 8$.

Then $T = \dfrac{8(16)}{16 - 8} = 16$.

c. 60 hours. See discussion in **a** above.

$.75h = 15$, so $h = 20$.

Then $L = \dfrac{20(30)}{30 - 20} = 60$.

d-e. See discussion in **a** above.

d. $4\frac{1}{2}$ hours. Lyle completed $\dfrac{1}{3}$ of the job in 5 hours, so it took 3 hours to do $\dfrac{2}{3}$ of the job together. Then $3 = .75(\dfrac{2}{3})(h)$, so $h = 6$. Then $.75(6) = 4.5$.

e. 10 hours. $T = \dfrac{6(15)}{15 - 6} = 10$.

f. Lyle 30 hrs., Theresa 10 hrs. See discussion in **a** above. Theresa did $\dfrac{2}{5}$ of the job in 4 hours, so it takes her 10 hours to do the job alone. From **a** above, $\dfrac{1}{L} + \dfrac{1}{T} = \dfrac{1}{h}$. Dividing both sides by $\dfrac{3}{4}$ and using $T = 10$, we have $\dfrac{4}{3}(\dfrac{1}{L} + \dfrac{1}{10}) = \dfrac{1}{\frac{3}{4}h}$, where $\dfrac{1}{\frac{3}{4}h}$ is the fraction of the job done in 1 hour when Lyle and Theresa are working together a 25% savings in efficiency. Then $\dfrac{3}{\frac{3}{4}h}$ is the fraction of the job done in 3 hours when they are working together at a 25% savings in efficiency. Lyle worked 2 hours alone, so we have $\dfrac{2}{L} + 3(\dfrac{4}{3})(\dfrac{1}{L} +$

$\dfrac{1}{10}) = \dfrac{3}{5}$. Solving, we get $L = 30$. To check, we can first take $\dfrac{1}{30} + \dfrac{1}{10} = \dfrac{1}{7\frac{1}{2}}$, showing the job takes $7\frac{1}{2}$ hours without accounting for the 25% efficiency savings. Then 75% of $7\frac{1}{2} = 5\frac{5}{8}$ hours the job actually takes when Lyle and Theresa work together, so they did $\dfrac{3}{5\frac{5}{8}}$ of the job when they worked for 3 hours. Working alone, Lyle did $\dfrac{2}{30}$ of the job, and Theresa did $\dfrac{4}{10}$ of the job, so we should have $\dfrac{2}{30} + \dfrac{3}{5\frac{5}{8}} + \dfrac{4}{10} = 1$, which is, in fact, true.

g-h. **g.** 8 hrs **h.** Lyle $22\frac{6}{7}$ hrs; Theresa 20 hrs. See discussion in **a** above. $\dfrac{9}{10} - \dfrac{2}{5} = \dfrac{1}{2}$ of the job was done in 4 hours of working together, so the whole job would take them 8 hours. Then in the first 2 hours Lyle helped, $\dfrac{1}{4}$ of the job would have been done, so $\dfrac{1}{4} + \dfrac{1}{2} = \dfrac{3}{4}$ of the job was done while Lyle was helping. Then Theresa did $\dfrac{9}{10} - \dfrac{3}{4} = \dfrac{3}{20}$ of the job in the 3 hours she worked alone, so it takes her 20 hours to do the job alone. $(\frac{3}{4})h = 8$, so $h = \frac{32}{3}$.

Referring again to the discussion in **a** above, we have $L = \dfrac{\frac{32}{3}(20)}{20 - \frac{32}{3}}$,

and so $L = \dfrac{160}{7}$ or $22\frac{6}{7}$ hours.

To check, we ask $\dfrac{3}{20} + 6(\frac{4}{3}) \cdot \left(\dfrac{1}{22\frac{6}{7}} + \dfrac{1}{20}\right) \overset{?}{=} \dfrac{9}{10}$ and we find

that it does.

MISCELLANEOUS

1. 41. $2n + 5 = 82$

2. 39 and 40. $n + (n + 1) = 79$

3. 74 and 76. $n + (n + 2) = 150$

4. 31 and 33. $n + (n + 2) = 64$

Note: When your students have done problems 3 and 4, ask how come one pair of answers was even and the other pair was odd, even though the equations for both problems use the same variables— i.e., n and $n + 2$.

5. 16. $3s = 48$

6. 15 cm. $80 = 2(25 + w)$

7. 18. $\dfrac{n}{2} + 3n = 63$

8. 6, 9, 15. $\dfrac{2}{10} = \dfrac{x}{30}$; $\dfrac{3}{10} = \dfrac{x}{30}$; $\dfrac{5}{10} = \dfrac{x}{30}$

9. 48. $\dfrac{3}{4}p = 36$

10. 18 cm each. $2s + 8 = 44$

11. 16. $2{,}500t = 20(2{,}000)$

12. a. 11 hrs. $t = 5 + \dfrac{300}{50}$

   b. $54\frac{6}{11}$ kph. $r = \dfrac{D}{t} = \dfrac{300 + 300}{11}$

13. 140. $.60t = 84$

14. 25, 26, 27. $n + (n + 1) + (n + 2) = 78$

15. 152 for soybeans, 38 for corn, 114 for wheat

   $\dfrac{4}{8} = \dfrac{x}{304}$; $\dfrac{1}{8} = \dfrac{x}{304}$; $\dfrac{3}{8} = \dfrac{x}{304}$

16. 32 and 34. $n + (n + 2) = 66$

17. 115. $.75p = 86.25$

18. 4. $n = 16\left(\dfrac{1}{n}\right)$

19. 1 cm. $A = s^2$. (Use this to find the side of each of the two squares.) Then space $= \dfrac{S_l - S_s}{2}$.

20. \$18,750. $.02t = 375$

21. a. \$105. $.79p = 82.95$

   b. \$22.05. $t = .21(105)$ OR $t = 105.00 - 82.95$

22. 16. $3n + \dfrac{1}{2}(3n) = 72$

23. 15 cm. $225 = \pi r^2$

24. a. 100°. $212 = \dfrac{9}{5}C + 32$

   b. 0°. $32 = \dfrac{9}{5}C + 32$

   c. 37°. $98.6 = \dfrac{9}{5}C + 32$

d. $26\frac{2}{3}°$ or more. $80 = \frac{9}{5}C + 32$

25. 15. $15(10) + 20h = 18(10 + h)$

26. 30. $60(10) + 80(c) = 75(10 + c)$

27. 16. $36(80) + 60t = 40(80 + t)$

28. 60. $.10p = 6$

29. a. $29,000. $26,680 = .92s$

    b. $2,320. $c = .08(29,000)$

30. a. $35,000. $1.08b = 37,800$

    b. $2,800. $c = .08(35,000)$

31. $36,000 and $24,000

$$\frac{6}{10} = \frac{x}{60,000}; \frac{4}{10} = \frac{x}{60,000}$$

32. –20. $\frac{n}{5} - 3 = \frac{n}{4} - 2$

33. 30. $120(10) + 160d = 150(10 + d)$

34. 8 hrs. $D = rt$. Masterson's rate

$$= \frac{150\text{km}}{6\text{hr}} = 25 \text{ kph. Then } 400 = 2(25)t.$$

35. 10 cm. $2w - l = 2(l + w) - 30$

36. a. $48,000. $\frac{1}{3} = \frac{x}{144,000}$

    b. $57,600; $38,400; $48,000.

$$\frac{12}{30} = \frac{x}{144,000}; \frac{8}{30} = \frac{x}{144,000};$$
$$\frac{10}{30} = \frac{x}{144,000}$$

    c. $72,000; $48,000; $24,000.

$$\frac{3}{6} = \frac{x}{144,000}; \frac{2}{6} = \frac{x}{144,000};$$
$$\frac{1}{6} = \frac{x}{144,000}$$

37. 5. $168(10) + 180g = 172(10 + g)$

38. 184. $168(10) + a(6) = 174(10 + 6)$

39. 3. $6.00s + 8.00(9) = 7.50(s + 9)$

40. a. 4. $80,000g + 60,000(12) =$
    $65,000(g + 12)$

    b. $75,000. $a(6) = 60,000(12) =$
    $65,000(6 + 12)$

41. 20 and 16. $\frac{n}{n - 4} = \frac{5}{4}$

42. –7 and –4. $\frac{n}{n + 3} = \frac{7}{4}$

43. $5\frac{1}{2}$%. $2,000(\frac{r}{100}) = 110.$ (OR, $2,000r$
    $= 110$, and then multiply r by 100 to
    convert to a percent.)

44. 7%. $2(\frac{r}{100})(2,350) = 329$

45. 30, 31, 32, 33
    $n + (n + 1) + (n + 2) + (n + 3) = 126$

46. $6.75 a pound
    $4(10) + s(12) = 5.50(22)$

47. 30. $1.2(10) + 1.6(m) = 1.5(10 + m)$

48. a. 120. $\frac{5}{6}n - \frac{3}{4}n = 10$

    b. 90. $\frac{3}{4}$ of 120

    c. 100. $\frac{5}{6}$ of 120

.he given formula, substituting
.ollows:

a. 64 ft. $s = 2$

b. 1,600 ft. $s = 10$

c. 57,600 ft. (almost 11 miles) $s = 60$

d. $2\frac{1}{2}$ sec. $f = 100$

e. $9\frac{1}{2}$ sec. $f = 1,454$

f. 9 sec. $f = 1,250$

g. 8 sec. $f = 984$

h. $46\frac{1}{2}$ sec. $f = 5,280(6\frac{1}{2})$

50. 76. $10(94) + 10(68) + 5a = 25(80)$

51. Notice that it is important to decide the order in which A, B, and C lie— i.e., ABC, ACB, or BAC. The given information is consistent only in the case of BAC (or CAB). Then the given information can be diagrammed as

$$\text{B} -\overset{x}{-} - - \text{A} -\overset{2x}{-} - - - \text{C}$$

and so

    a. 60 miles. $3x = 180$

    b. 120 miles. $D = 2x = 2(60)$

52. 72 and 75. $3n + 3(n + 1) = 147$

53. 84. $5(100) + 20(80) = 25a$

54. 9%. $.06(4,000) + \frac{r}{100}(2,000) = 420$

55. $93.75. $s - 75 = .20s$

56. **a.** $78. $s = 1.30(60)$

    b. $105. $136.50 = 1.30c$

57. $15,000
$10(25,000) + 20(10,000) + 70a = 100(15,000)$

58. 3 nickels, 8 dimes
$n + d = 11$
$5n + 10d = 95$

59. Luke is 16, Marian is 11
$L = M + 5$
$L + M = 27$

60. 42 and 27
$a = b + 15$
$a + b = 69$

61. Frances is 62 in. tall; Juan is 65 in. tall.
$J = F + 3$
$J + F = 127$

62. **a.** 3,478 yd **b.** 3,778 yd
$f + s = 7,256$
$s = f + 300$

63. razor 80¢, blades 30¢
$r + b = 1.10$
$r = b + .50$

64. boots $7, shoes $11
$s + b = 18$
$s = b + 4$

65. 54 and 27
$a = 2b$
$a + b = 81$

66. width 10 cm, length 15 cm
$w = \frac{2}{3}l$
$2(w + l) = 50$

67. 485 juniors, 350 seniors
$j = s + 135$
$j + s = 835$

68. **a.** 30   **b.** 20
$r = w + 10$
$r + w = 50$

69. 50 nickels, 47 pennies
$n = p + 3$
$p + 5n = 297$

70. 2 full-page, 8 half-page
$f + h = 10$
$700f + 400h = 4,600$

71. 41 and 14
$a + b = 55$
$a - b = 27$

72. **a.** 10¢   **b.** 65¢
$p + d = 75$
$d = p - 55$

73. width 8 cm, length 11 cm
$l = w + 3$
$38 = 2(l + w)$

74. $14\frac{1}{2}$ and $-7\frac{1}{2}$
$a + b = 7$
$a - b = 22$

75. 10 horses, 90 chickens
$h + c = 100$
$4h + 2c = 220$

76. **a.** 568   **b.** 619
$f + s = 1,187$
$s = f + 51$

77. **a.** 8 cm   **b.** 3 cm
$2l + b = 19$
$l = b + 5$

78. -3. $2x + 3 = x$

79. 15¢ for the apple, 25¢ for the orange
$a + g = 40$
$g = a + 10$

80. 17 and 20
$5a - 3b = 25$
$a + b = 37$

81. Dinah is 7, Mario is 19. Notice that the second statement makes Mario older than Dinah.

$(M - 1) - (D + 1) = 10$
$M + 5 = 2(D + 5)$

82. 8 by A, 11 by B
$A + B = 19$
$10A + 6B = 146$

83. 10 pennants, 40 T shirts
$p + t = 50$
$3.50p + 6t = 275$

84. $f + h = 18$

   a. \$6 fishing, \$12 hunting. $h = 2f$

   b. \$7 fishing, \$11 hunting. $h = f + 4$

   c. \$5 fishing, \$13 hunting. $2f = h - 3$

   d. One license was \$4 and the other was \$14, but not enough information is given to determine which is which.
   $f - h = 10$ OR $h - f = 10$

85. 10 units by 22 units
$l - 2w = 2$
$2(l + w) = 64$

86. 74
$t + u = 11$
$u = t - 3$

87. $h + c = 300$
   a. \$175 cow, \$125 horse. $c = h + 50$

   b. \$225 cow, \$75 horse. $c = 3h$

   c. \$175 cow, \$125 horse. $2h - c = 75$

   d. One was \$115 and the other was \$185, but not enough information is given to determine which is which. $h - c = 70$ OR $c - h = 70$

88. The area becomes six times as great. $A = lw$, so
   a. $(2l)(3w) = 6lw = 6A$

   b. $(3l)(2w) = 6lw = 6A$

ese, 20 sheep

_s = 30

_g + 4s = 100

-5. $3x + 10 = x$

a. 24   **b.** 2,016

$84n = t$

$96(n - 3) = t$

92. 53

$t + u = 8$

$(10t + u) - (10u + t) = 18$

93. a. 3 ft. $8s^2 = 72$

b. 6 ft. by 12 ft. $3 = \frac{1}{2}w$

$wl = 72$

94. 12. $x = \frac{x}{3} + 8$

95. $b + g = 30$

a. 17 boys, 13 girls. $b = g + 4$

b. 10 boys, 20 girls. $g = 2b$

c. 6 boys, 24 girls. $b = .25g$

d. 12 boys, 18 girls. $b = g - 6$

96. 95 or 59

$t + u = 14$

$t - u = 4$ or $u - t = 4$

97. first man 178, anchor man 225

$f + a = 403$

$a = f + 47$

98. $1\frac{1}{6}$ and $\frac{1}{3}$. $\frac{a + b}{2} = \frac{3}{4}$

$a - b = \frac{5}{6}$

99. 20 @ \$10 = \$200; 40 @ \$16 = \$640; 60 @ \$20 = \$1,200.

$10(\frac{n}{6}) + 16(\frac{n}{3}) + 20(n - \frac{n}{6} - \frac{n}{3}) = 2,040$

$n = 120$, so $10(\frac{120}{6}) = 10(20)$;

$16(\frac{120}{3}) = 16(40)$;

$20(120 - \frac{120}{6} - \frac{120}{3}) = 20(60)$

100. a. \$5   **b.** \$2. $r = d + 3$

$2d + r = 9$

101. a. 260   **b.** 190. $h + v = 500 - 50$

$h = v + 70$

102. Garnet is 9, Jeremy is 7

$G + 5 = 2J$

$J = G - 2$

103. a. 3,000. $1,000 = c - \frac{1}{2}c - \frac{1}{3}(c - \frac{1}{2}c)$

b. 1,500. $\frac{1}{2}$ of 3,000

c. 500. $\frac{1}{3}$ of (3,000 - 1,500)

104. a. 1,500   **b.** 1,200

$s + d = 2,700$

$.05s + .15d = 255$

105. Irene is 14, Jerry is 16

$J - 1 + 5 + 2I = 48$

$J = I + 2$

106. \$30 cow, \$60 horse

$h = 2c$

$h + c = 90$

107. 10 @ \$3, 4 @ \$4

$f + t = 14$

$4f + 3t = 46$

108. a. \$2.38 a lb. x 3 lb. = \$7.14.

b. 98¢ a loaf x 2 loaves = \$1.96.

$3c + 2b = 910$

$c = b + 140$

109. a. 12 apples, 8 oranges

$a + g = 20$

$15a + 20g = 340$

b. 20 apples, 14 oranges
$a = g + 6$
$15a + 20g = 580$

c. 18 apples, 36 oranges
$g = 2a$
$15a + 20g = 990$

110. 45 and 15
$a = 3b$
$ab = 675$

111. 6 and 12. Since the sum of the ages is more than twice one of the ages, one child is younger than the other, and it is this child whose age must be less than half the sum at any given time. Put y = the current age (in years) of the younger child. Put e = the current age (in years) of the elder child. Then
$y + e = 3y$ and $(y - 3) + (e - 3) = 4(y - 3)$

112. $46\frac{6}{19}$ mph. $t = \dfrac{D}{r}$, $r = \dfrac{D}{t}$, so

$$r = \frac{100 + 100}{\dfrac{100}{40} + \dfrac{100}{55}}$$

113. 72 and 9
$a + b = 81$
$\dfrac{a}{b} = 8$

114. $\dfrac{2}{7}$ liter
$.90(1) + 0w = .70(1 + w)$ OR
$.10(1) + 1.00w = .30(1 + w)$

115. 76 and 38 OR –76 and –38
$a = 2b$
$a - b = 38$ OR $b - a = 38$

116. 12 dimes, 6 quarters
$d + q = 18$
$10d + 25q = 270$

117. Loquacia is 12, Mortimer
$L^2 - (L - 5)^2 = 95$

118. 5 $4x - 15 = x$

119. 7 and 25 or $28\frac{3}{5}$ and $10\frac{3}{5}$.
$2a + 3b = 89, a - b = 18$ OR
$2a + 3b = 89, b - a = 18$

120. $Z = 2U$
$Z = Y - 5$

a. $U + Y + Z = 35$

b. $U + Y = 20$

c. $Z - U = 8$

d. $Y - U = 16$

e. $U + Z = 21$

f. $Y + Z = 17$

g. $Y = U + 13$

Ulysses	Yolanda	Zinnia
6	17	12
5	15	10
8	21	16
11	27	22
7	19	14
3	11	6
8	21	16